STUDY EDITION:
The Emerald Tablets
of Thoth The Atlantean

With Easy Chapter and Verse Format

Rebecca Marina Messenger

STUDY EDITION:
The Emerald Tablets of Thoth The Atlantean
With Easy Chapter and Verse Format

Copyright 2020 by Rebecca Marina Messenger

All rights reserved. No part of this publication may be reproduced, distributed, or transmitted in any form or by any means, including photocopying, recording, or other electronic or mechanical methods, without the prior written permission of the publisher, except in the case of brief quotations embodied in critical reviews and certain other noncommercial uses permitted by copyright law. For permission requests, email the publisher at Rebecca@rebeccamarina.com

ISBN: 978-0-9759390-3-1 (E-Book)
ISBN: 978-0-9759390-4-8 (Print)

Published by Celebration Healing Publishing

Book Interior and E-book Design by Amit Dey | amitdey2528@gmail.com

FREE GIFT

Meditation from Thoth:
Flower of Fire blessing and cleansing.
WWW. Rebeccamarina.com/resources

Original Translation & Interpretation by Doreal

(Originally published in mimeographed form in the 1930's by a mysterious "Dr. Doreal," these writings quickly became an underground sensation among esotericists of the time. Tablets 1-13 are part of the original work. Tablets 14 and 15 are supplemental.

No one has ever seen the original tablets mentioned here, and in all likelihood, these writings would be considered channeled material today.

However, the Emerald Tablets of Thoth, the Atlantean, are still part of the modern Corpus Hermeticum, for they elaborate and deepen the meaning of the historical Emerald Tablets and writings of Thoth/Hermes.)

Table of Contents

Preface: Why this Format xi

How to use this Book xiii

Dedication. xvii

Acknowledgements. xix

Introduction to the Original Work by Doreal xxi

Chapter One:
Tablet One: The History of Thoth, the Atlantean . . . 1

Chapter Two:
Tablet Two: The Halls of Amenti 13

Chapter Three:
Tablet Three: The Key of Wisdom 25

Chapter Four:
Tablet Four: The Space Born. 37

Chapter Five:
Tablet Five: The Dweller of Unal 47

Chapter Six:
Tablet Six: The Key of Magic. 59

Table of Contents

Chapter Seven:
Tablet Seven: The Seven Lords.............. 71

Chapter Eight:
Tablet Eight: The Key of Mysteries 83

Chapter Nine:
Tablet Nine: The Key of Freedom of Space...... 95

Chapter Ten:
Tablet Ten: The Key of Time 107

Chapter Eleven:
Tablet Eleven: The Key to Above and Below.... 119

Chapter Twelve:
Tablet Twelve: The Law of Cause and Effect and the Key of Prophecy 131

Chapter Thirteen:
Tablet Thirteen: The Keys of Life and Death 141

Chapter Fourteen:
Tablet Fourteen: Becoming Thrice Great........ 151

Chapter Fifteen:
Tablet Fifteen: Secret of Secrets 165

Chapter Sixteen:
Index of Common Search Terms.............. 173

Chapter Seventeen:
Index of Power Prayers..................... 181

Table of Contents

Chapter Eighteen:
Index of Power Words 183

Chapter Nineteen:
Index of Techniques 187

Chapter Twenty:
Meditations Inspired by the Emerald Tablets . . . 199

Chapter Twenty-one:
How Thoth Built the Great Pyramid 215

Chapter Twenty-two:
Are You A Keymaster of the Emerald Tablets? . . 219

Chapter Twenty-three:
Thoth on Judgment 223

References 227

About the Author 229

Preface

Why this Format

This book is presented in chapter and verse format like the Holy Scriptures.

This makes it easy for a group to study together, no matter if the copy is print, Kindle or E-book.

Page numbers may change but chapter and verse are always the same.

In this time of awakening, groups of seekers are beginning to study these tablets together. It is our hope that this format makes it easier to come together.

Chapter and verse format also breaks up long paragraphs into more digestible bites, and the larger font makes it easy on the eyes.

Not one word of the original text by Doreal has been changed!

Yes, there are commentaries and references, yet these are in different fonts, and it's very clear which is the original and which is the comment.

How to use this Book

Reading The Emerald Tablets will unlock the Light within you! It is recommended to read small sections at a time.

Space has been purposefully left for you to make your own comments. **When you have a question or don't agree with something...write it down!** There is no big evil God-King waiting to strike you down!

You learn most by asking questions. Fear is the enemy of growth!

Just ask and be still...as you are ready, revelation will come to you. Be not afraid.

You would NOT be attracted to this material at all, if you are not already a chosen one. Yes, your soul is choosing to be part of the Great Awakening, in whatever capacity is right for you.

Relax and read!

How to use this Book

As Doreal himself said…
Read. Believe or not, but read. And the vibration found therein will awaken a response in your soul!

> *Comment from Rebecca. There are several instances where I did not "like" what I was reading…I simply made a note of it and left it alone. A good teacher invites students to question and have an opinion. All will be made clear when it is needed.*

The following prayer will bring in the assistance of Thoth himself, to guide you in understanding all that your heart is ready for.

Prayer of Thoth

T12, V24-25.
Receive thou my blessing.
Take thou my way and follow the Light.
Blend thou thy Soul in the Great Essence.
ONE with the Great Light let thy consciousness be.
Call thou on me when thou dost need me.
Use my name three times in a row:
CHEQUETET, ARELICH, VOMALITES.

Sounds like:
Che que tet - - Cha-kwet-tet
Are lich - - Are-lick
Vo mal i tes - - Vo-mol-e-tess

I ask Thoth: Please guide me in the understanding of all that I am ready for. Let understanding and revelation come in increments that are for my highest good. Amen.

One final Tip for getting the MOST from these Tablets.

Read them aloud!

Did you know that Abe Lincoln read the newspaper aloud in his booming voice every morning? When asked why he read aloud, he replied: "When I read aloud, two senses catch the idea: first I SEE what I read; second, I HEAR it, and therefore I can remember it better."

Add to that the power of sound vibration these words are creating.

Speaking aloud utilizes the throat chakra, adding the power of the spoken word. Thoth speaks often of the power of WORDS. References to "WORD" occur almost 90 times in these Tablets.

Dedication

This book is respectfully dedicated to Thoth the Atlantean, and Thotme, father of Thoth, a most joyous energy.

To Doreal, utmost respect and admiration for following your guidance when it seemed impossible!

To the couple who held the translations in secret for many years. (names unknown)

And to the very brave woman who survived the jungle, traveled far, and retrieved the translations so that they could be had by millions of awakening hearts. (name unknown)

Also, in respect and admiration, this format is dedicated to Drunvalo Melchizedek for his pioneering work.

To Billy Carson for bringing the awareness of Thoth to thousands.

To my main squeeze, Sri Yukteswar, for bringing this awareness full circle.

...and finally, to YOU, the seeker.

May your heart be more fully opened, and may the flower of life flame brightly within you!

Acknowledgements

Heartfelt thanks to Lee Wolf for her tireless efforts in helping to edit. Her "eagle eyes" were invaluable in getting this out to the world. I love you, Lee.

Thanks to my friend Cindy Cook, who made it seem like doing a book was the simplest thing in the world.

Thanks to all my readers and YouTube followers, for expressing such interest in The Emerald Tablets!

Introduction to the Original Work by Doreal

In the following pages, I will reveal some of the mysteries which, as yet, have only been touched upon lightly, either by myself, or by other teachers or students of truth.

Man's search, for the understanding of laws which regulate his life, has been unending. Yet, just beyond the veil which shields the higher planes from material man's vision, the truth has always existed. It is ready to be assimilated by those who enlarge their vision by turning inward, not outward, in their search.

In the silence of material senses, lies the key to the unveiling of wisdom. He who talks does not know; he who knows does not talk. The highest knowledge is unutterable, for it exists as an entity in lanes which transcend all material words or symbols.

All symbols are but keys to doors leading to truths. Many times the doors are not opened, because the keys seem so great, that the things which are beyond, are not visible.

We need to understand that all keys, all material symbols, are manifestations, which are but extensions of a great law and truth. Then we will begin to develop the vision which will enable us to penetrate beyond the veil.

All things in all universes, move according to law. This law, which regulates the movement of the planets, is no more immutable, than the law which regulates the material expressions of man.

One of the greatest of all Cosmic Laws is that which is responsible for the formation of man as a material being. The great aim of the mystery schools of all ages, has been to reveal the workings of the law which connect man, the material, and man, the spiritual.

The connecting link between the material man and the spiritual man, is the intellectual man, for the mind partakes of both the material and immaterial qualities.

The aspirant for higher knowledge must develop the intellectual side of his nature, and so strengthen his will, that it is able to concentrate all powers of his being on, and in, the plane he desires.

The great search for light, life and love, only begins on the material plane. Carried to its ultimate, its final goal is complete oneness with the Universal

Introduction to the Original Work

Consciousness. The foundation in the material is the first step; then comes the higher goal of spiritual attainment.

In the following pages, I will give an interpretation of the Emerald Tablets and their secret, hidden and esoteric meanings. Concealed in the words of Thoth, are many meanings that do not appear on the surface. The light of knowledge brought to bear by the Tablets, will open many new fields for thought.

"Read and be wise," but only if the light of your own consciousness, awakens the deep-seated understanding, which is an inherent quality of the soul.

In the Threefold Light, Doreal's PREFACE to the Emerald Tablets of Thoth, the Atlantean:

The history of the Tablets, translated in the following pages, is strange and beyond the belief of modern scientists. Their antiquity is stupendous, dating back some 36,000 years B.C. The writer is Thoth, an Atlantean Priest-King, who founded a colony in ancient Egypt, after the sinking of the mother country.

He was the builder of the Great Pyramid of Giza, erroneously attributed to Cheops. (See The Great Pyramid by Doreal.)

In it, he incorporated his knowledge of the ancient wisdom, and also securely secreted records and instruments of ancient Atlantis.

For some 16,000 years, he ruled the ancient race of Egypt, from approximately 50,000 B.C. to 36,000 B.C. At that time, the ancient barbarous race, among which he and his followers had settled, had been raised to a high degree of civilization.

Thoth was an immortal, that is, he had conquered death, passing only when he willed, and even then not through death. His vast wisdom made him ruler over the various Atlantean colonies, including the ones in South and Central America.

When the time came for him to leave Egypt, he erected the Great Pyramid over the entrance to the Great Halls of Amenti, placed in it his records, and appointed guards for his secrets from among the highest of his people.

In later times, in the age of darkness which followed his passing, descendants of these guards became the pyramid priests. They deified Thoth as the God of Wisdom, The Recorder. In legend, the Halls of Amenti became the underworld, the Halls of the Gods, where the soul passed after death for judgment.

Introduction to the Original Work

During later ages, the ego of Thoth passed into the bodies of men in the manner described in the Tablets. As such, he incarnated three times. In his last, he was known as Hermes, the thrice-born. In this incarnation, he left the writings known to modern occultists as the Emerald Tablets, a later and far lesser exposition, of the ancient mysteries.

The Tablets translated in this work, are ten which were left in the Great Pyramid, in the custody of the pyramid priests. The ten are divided into thirteen parts for the sake of convenience.

The last two are so great and far-reaching in their import that at present, it is forbidden to release them to the world at large. However, in those contained herein, are secrets which will prove of inestimable value to the serious student.

They should be read, not once, but a hundred times, for only thus can the true meaning be revealed. A casual reading will give glimpses of beauty, but more intensive study will open avenues of wisdom to the seeker.

But now a word as to how these mighty secrets came to be revealed to modern man after being hidden for so long: Some thirteen hundred years B.C., Egypt, the ancient Khem, was in turmoil, and many delegations of priests were sent to other parts of the world.

Among these were some of the pyramid priests, who carried with them the Emerald Tablets, as a talisman by which they could exercise authority over the less-advanced priest-craft of races descended from other Atlantean colonies.

The Tablets were understood from legend, to give the bearer authority from Thoth.

The particular group of priests bearing the tablets emigrated to South America, where they found a flourishing race, the Mayans, who remembered much of the ancient wisdom.

Among these, the priests settled and remained. In the tenth century, the Mayans had thoroughly settled the Yucatan, and the tablets were placed beneath the altar of one of the great temples of the Sun God.

After the conquest of the Mayans by the Spaniards, the cities were abandoned, and the treasures of the temples forgotten.

It should be understood that the Great Pyramid of Egypt has been, and still is, a temple of initiation into the mysteries. Jesus, Solomon, Apollonius and others, were initiated there.

The writer (who has a connection with the Great White Lodge, which also works through the pyramid priesthood) was instructed to recover and return the ancient Tablets to the Great Pyramid. This, after adventures which need not be detailed here, was accomplished.

Before returning them, he was given permission to translate and retain a copy of the wisdom engraved on the Tablets. This was done in 1925, and only now has permission been given for part to be published.

It is expected that many will scoff. Yet the true student will read between the lines, and gain wisdom. If the light is in you, the light which is engraved in these Tablets, will respond.

Now, a word as to the material aspect of the Tablets: They consist of twelve Tablets of emerald green, which were formed from a substance created through alchemical transmutation. They are imperishable, and resistant to all elements and substances. In effect, the atomic and cellular structure is fixed, so that no change can ever take place.

In this respect, the Tablets violate the material law of ionization. Upon them are engraved characters in the ancient Atlantean language. These are characters which respond to attuned thought waves, releasing the associated mental vibration in the mind of the reader.

The Tablets are fastened together with hoops of golden-colored alloy, suspended from a rod of the same material. So much for the material appearance.

The wisdom contained therein, is the foundation of the ancient mysteries. And for the one who reads with open eyes and mind, his wisdom shall be increased a hundred-fold.

Read. Believe or not, but read. And the vibration found therein will awaken a response in your soul!

In Cosmic Harmony,
Doreal, Supreme Voice of the Brotherhood.

Chapter One

Emerald Tablet One:
The History of Thoth, the Atlantean

Tablet 1, Verse 1.
I, THOTH, the Atlantean,
master of mysteries, keeper of records,
mighty king, magician,
living from generation to generation,
being about to pass into the Halls of Amenti,
set down for the guidance
of those that are to come after,
these records of the mighty wisdom of
Great Atlantis.

T1, V2.
In the great city of KEOR,
on the island of UNDAL
in a time far past, I began this incarnation.
Not as the little men of the present age
did the mighty ones of Atlantis live and die,
but rather from aeon to aeon
did they renew their life in the Halls of Amenti
where the river of life flows eternally onward.

T1, V3.
A hundred times ten
have I descended the dark way that led into light,
and as many times have I ascended
from the darkness into the light,
my strength and power renewed.

T1, V4.
Now for a time I descend,
and the men of KHEM shall know me no more.
But in a time yet unborn
will I rise again, mighty and potent,
requiring an accounting of those left behind me.

T1, V5.
Then beware, O men of KHEM,
if ye have falsely betrayed my teaching,
for I shall cast ye down from your high estate
into the darkness of the caves
from whence ye came.
Betray not my secrets to the men of the North
or the men of the South lest my curse fall upon ye.

T1, V6.
Remember and heed my words,
for surely will I return again
and require of thee that which ye guard.
Aye, even from beyond time
and from beyond death will I return,

rewarding or punishing
as ye have requited your trust.

T1,V7.
Great were my people in the ancient days,
great beyond the conception
of the little people now around me;
knowing the wisdom of old,
seeking far within the heart of infinity
knowledge that belonged to Earth's youth.
Wise were we with the wisdom
of the Children of Light who dwelt among us.
Strong were we with the power
drawn from the eternal fire.

T1, V8.
And of all these,
greatest among the children of men
was my father, THOTME,
keeper of the great temple,
link between the Children of Light
who dwelt within the temple and
the races of men who inhabited the ten islands.

T1, V9.
Mouthpiece, after the Three,
of the Dweller of UNAL,
speaking to the Kings
with the voice that must be obeyed.

T1, V10.
Grew I there from a child into manhood,
being taught by my father the elder mysteries,
until in time there grew within, the fire of wisdom,
until it burst into a consuming flame.

T1, V11.
Naught desired I but the attainment of wisdom.
Until on a great day
the command came from the Dweller of the Temple
that I be brought before him.
Few there were among the children of men who
had looked upon that mighty face and lived, for not
as the sons of men are the Children of Light
when they are not incarnate in a physical body.

T1, V12.
Chosen was I from the sons of men,
taught by the Dweller
so that his purposes might be fulfilled,
purposes yet unborn in the womb of time.

T1, V13.
Long ages I dwelt in the Temple,
learning ever and yet ever more wisdom,
until I, too, approached the light
emitted from the great fire.

Tablet One

T1, V14.
Taught me he, the path to Amenti,
the underworld where the great king
sits upon his throne of might.
Deep I bowed in homage
before the Lords of Life and the Lords of Death,
receiving as my gift the Key of Life.

T1, V15.
Free was I of the Halls of Amenti,
bound not by death to the circle of life.
Far to the stars I journeyed
until space and time became as naught.
Then having drunk deep of the cup of wisdom,
I looked into the hearts of men
and there found I greater mysteries and was glad.
For only in the Search for Truth
could my Soul be stilled
and the flame within be quenched.

> (Commentary: After traveling far to the stars, and being freed from the Halls of Amenti, Thoth still finds the greater mystery in the hearts of men.)

T1, V16.
Down through the ages I lived,
seeing those around me taste of the cup of death
and return again in the light of life.

Gradually from the Kingdoms of Atlantis
passed waves of consciousness
that had been one with me,
only to be replaced by spawn of a lower star.

T1, V17.
In obedience to the law,
the word of the Master grew into flower.
Downward into darkness
turned the thoughts of the Atlanteans,
Until at last in his wrath
arose from his AGWANTI, the Dweller,
(this word has no English equivalent;
it means a state of detachment)
speaking The Word, calling the power.
Deep in Earth's heart,
the sons of Amenti heard, and hearing,
directed the changing
of the flower of fire that burns eternally,
changing and shifting, using the LOGOS,
until that great fire changed its direction.

T1, V18.
Over the world then broke the great waters,
drowning and sinking, changing Earth's balance
until only the Temple of Light was left standing
on the great mountain on UNDAL
still rising out of the water;
some there were who were living,
saved from the rush of the fountains.

T1, V19.
Called to me then the Master, saying:
"Gather ye together my people.
Take them by the arts ye have learned of
far across the waters,
until ye reach the land of the hairy barbarians,
dwelling in caves of the desert.
Follow there the plan that ye know of."

T1, V20.
Gathered I then my people
and entered the great ship of the Master.
Upward we rose into the morning.
Dark beneath us lay the Temple.
Suddenly over it rose the waters.
Vanished from Earth, until the time appointed,
was the great Temple.

T1, V21.
Fast we fled toward the sun of the morning,
until beneath us lay the land
of the children of KHEM.
Raging, they came with cudgels
and spears lifted in anger
seeking to slay and utterly destroy
the Sons of Atlantis.

T1, V22.
Then raised I my staff
and directed a ray of vibration,

striking them still in their tracks
as fragments of stone of the mountain.
Then spoke I to them
in words calm and peaceful,
telling them of the might of Atlantis,
saying we were children of the Sun
and its messengers.
Cowed I them by my display of magic-science,
until at my feet they groveled,
when I released them.

T1, V23.
Long dwelt we in the land of KHEM,
long and yet long again.
Until obeying the commands of the Master,
who while sleeping yet lives eternally,
I sent from me the Sons of Atlantis,
sent them in many directions,
that from the womb of time
wisdom might rise again in her children.

T1, V24.
Long time dwelt I in the land of KHEM,
doing great works by the wisdom within me.
Upward grew into the light of knowledge
the children of KHEM,
watered by the rains of my wisdom.
Blasted I then a path to Amenti
so that I might retain my powers,

living from age to age a Sun of Atlantis,
keeping the wisdom, preserving the records.

T1, V25.
Great grew the sons of KHEM,
conquering the people around them,
growing slowly upwards in Soul force.
Now for a time I go from among them
into the dark halls of Amenti,
deep in the halls of the Earth,
before the Lords of the Powers,
face to face once again with the Dweller.

T1, V26.
Raised I high over the entrance, a doorway,
a gateway leading down to Amenti.
Few there would be with courage to dare it,
few pass the portal to dark Amenti.
Raised over the passage, I, a mighty pyramid,
using the power
that overcomes Earth force (*gravity*).
Deep and yet deeper placed I
a force-house or chamber;
from it carved I a circular passage
reaching almost to the great summit.
There in the apex, set I the crystal,
sending the ray into the "Time-Space,"
drawing the force from out of the ether,
concentrating upon the gateway to Amenti.
(*See "The Great Pyramid" by Doreal.*)

T1, V27.
Other chambers I built
and left vacant to all seeming,
yet hidden within them are the keys to Amenti.
He who in courage would dare the dark realms,
let him be purified first by long fasting.
Lie in the sarcophagus of stone in my chamber.
Then reveal I to him the great mysteries.
Soon shall he follow to where I shall meet him,
even in the darkness of Earth shall I meet him,
I, Thoth, Lord of Wisdom,
meet him and hold him and dwell with him always.

T1, V28.
Builded I the Great Pyramid,
patterned after the pyramid of Earth force,
burning eternally so that it, too,
might remain through the ages.
In it, I builded my knowledge of "Magic-Science"
so that it might be here
when again I return from Amenti.
Aye, while I sleep in the Halls of Amenti,
my Soul roaming free will incarnate,
dwell among men in this form or another.
(*Hermes, thrice-born.*)

T1, V29.
Emissary on Earth am I of the Dweller,
fulfilling his commands so man might be lifted.
Now return I to the Halls of Amenti,

leaving behind me some of my wisdom.
Preserve ye and keep ye
the command of the Dweller:
Lift ever upwards your eyes toward the light.
Surely in time, ye are one with the Master,
surely by right ye are one with the Master,
surely by right ye are one with the ALL.

T1, V30.
Now, I depart from ye.
Know my commandments,
keep them and be them,
and I will be with you,
helping and guiding you into the Light.

Now before me opens the portal.
Go I down in the darkness of night.

(Comment by Thoth: Though sleeping my body may be, yet my consciousness is always roaming. It is always available to those who call to me with pureness of heart.)

NOTES

Chapter Two

Emerald Tablet Two:
The Halls of Amenti

Tablet 2, Verse1.
Deep in Earth's heart lie the Halls of Amenti,
far 'neath the islands of sunken Atlantis,
Halls of the Dead and Halls of the Living,
bathed in the fire of the infinite ALL.

T2, V2.
Far in a past time, lost in the space-time,
the Children of Light looked down on the world.
Seeing the children of men in their bondage,
bound by the force that came from beyond.
Knew they that only by freedom from bondage
could man ever rise from the Earth to the Sun.

T2, V3.
Down they descended and created bodies,
taking the semblance of men as their own.
The Masters of everything said after their forming:
"We are they who were formed from the space-dust,

partaking of life from the infinite ALL;
living in the world as children of men,
like and yet unlike the children of men."

T2, V4.
Then for a dwelling place,
far 'neath the Earth's crust,
blasted great spaces they by their power,
spaces apart from the children of men.
Surrounded them by forces and power,
shielded from harm they the Halls of the Dead.

T2, V5.
Side by side then, placed they other spaces,
filled them with Life and with Light from above.
Builded they then the Halls of Amenti,
that they might dwell eternally there
living with life to eternity's end.

T2, V6.
Thirty and two were there of the children,
sons of Light who had come among men,
seeking to free from the bondage of darkness
those who were bound by the force from beyond.

T2, V7.
Deep in the Halls of Life grew a flower,
flaming, expanding, driving backward the night.
Placed in the center, a ray of great potence,

Life giving, Light giving,
Filling with power all who came near it.

T2, V8.
Placed they around it thrones, two and thirty,
places for each of the Children of Light,
placed so that they were bathed in the radiance,
filled with the Life from the eternal Light.

T2, V9.
There time after time
placed they their first created bodies
so that they might be filled
with the Spirit of Life.
One hundred years out of each thousand
must the Life-giving Light
flame forth on their bodies.
Quickening, awakening the Spirit of Life.

T2, V10.
There in the circle from aeon to aeon,
sit the Great Masters,
living a life not known among men.
There in the Halls of Life they lie sleeping;
free flows their Soul through the bodies of men.
Time after time, while their bodies lie sleeping,
incarnate they in the bodies of men.
Teaching and guiding onward and upward,
out of the darkness into the Light.

Tablet Two

T2, V11.
There in the Hall of Life, filled with their wisdom,
known not to the races of man,
living forever 'neath the cold fire of life,
sit the Children of Light.
Times there are when they awaken,
come from the depths to be lights among men,
infinite they among finite men.

T2, V12.
He who by progress has grown from the darkness,
lifted himself from the night into light,
free is he made of the Halls of Amenti,
free of the Flower of Light and of Life.
Guided he then, by wisdom and knowledge,
passes from men, to the Master of Life.
There he may dwell as one with the Masters,
free from the bonds of the darkness of night.

T2, V13.
Seated within the flower of radiance
sit seven Lords from the Space-Times above us,
helping and guiding through infinite Wisdom,
the pathway through time of the children of men.
Mighty and strange, they, veiled with their power,
silent, all-knowing, drawing the Life force,
different yet one with the children of men.
Aye, different, and yet one
with the Children of Light.

T2, V14.
Custodians and watchers
of the force of man's bondage,
ready to loose when the light has been reached.
First and most mighty, sits the Veiled Presence,
Lord of Lords, the infinite Nine,
over the others from each Cosmic cycle,
weighing and watching the progress of men.

Under HE, sit the Lords of the Cycles;
Three, Four, Five, and Six, Seven, Eight,
each with his mission, each with his powers,
guiding, directing the destiny of man.

T2, V15.
There sit they, mighty and potent,
free of all time and space.
Not of this world they,
yet akin to it, Elder Brothers they,
of the children of men.
Judging and weighing, they with their wisdom,
watching the progress of Light among men.

T2, V16.
There before them was I led by the Dweller,
watched him blend with ONE from above.
Then from HE came forth a voice saying:
"Great art thou, Thoth, among children of men.
Free henceforth of the Halls of Amenti,

*Master of Life among children of men.
Taste not of death except as thou will it,
drink thou of Life to Eternity's end.
Henceforth forever is Life, thine for the taking.
Henceforth is Death at the call of thy hand.
Dwell here or leave here when thou desireth,
free is Amenti to the Sun of man.*

*T2, V17.
Take thou up Life in what form thou desireth,
Child of the Light that has grown among men.
Choose thou thy work, for all souls must labor,
never be free from the pathway of Light.
One step thou has gained
on the long pathway upward,
infinite now is the mountain of Light.
Each step thou taketh but heightens the mountain;
all of thy progress but lengthens the goal.
Approach ye ever the infinite Wisdom,
ever before thee recedes the goal.*

*T2, V18.
Free are ye made now of the Halls of Amenti
to walk hand in hand with the Lords of the world,
one in one purpose, working together,
bringers of Light to the children of men."*

*T2, V19.
Then from his throne came one of the Masters,
taking my hand and leading me onward,*

through all the Halls of the deep hidden land.
Led he me through the Halls of Amenti,
showing the mysteries that are known not to man.
Through the dark passage, downward he led me
into the Hall where sits the dark Death.
Vast as space lay the great Hall before me,
walled by darkness but yet filled with Light.

T2, V20.
Before me arose a great throne of darkness,
veiled on it seated a figure of night.
Darker than darkness sat the great figure,
dark with a darkness not of the night.
Before it then paused the Master,
speaking The Word that brings about Life, saying:

T2, V21.
"Oh, master of darkness,
guide of the way from Life unto Life,
before thee I bring a Sun of the morning.
Touch him not ever with the power of night.
Call not his flame to the darkness of night.
Know him, and see him, one of our brothers,
lifted from darkness into the Light.
Release thou his flame from its bondage,
free let it flame through the darkness of night."

T2, V22.
Raised then the hand of the figure,
forth came a flame that grew clear and bright.

Rolled back swiftly the curtain of darkness,
unveiled the Hall from the darkness of night.
Then grew in the great space before me,
flame after flame, from the veil of the night.
Uncounted millions leaped they before me,
some flaming forth as flowers of fire.

T2, V23.
Others there were that shed a dim radiance,
glowing but faintly from out of the night.
Some there were that faded swiftly;
others that grew from a small spark of light.
Each surrounded by its dim veil of darkness,
yet flaming with the light
that could never be quenched.
Coming and going like fireflies in springtime,
filled they the space with Light and with Life.

T2,V24.
Then spoke a voice, mighty and solemn, saying:
"These are lights that are souls among men,
growing and fading, existing forever,
changing yet living, through death into life.
When they have bloomed into flower,
reached the zenith of growth in their life,
swiftly then send I my veil of darkness,
shrouding and changing to new forms of life.
Steadily upward throughout the ages,
growing, expanding into yet greater flame,

*lighting the darkness with yet greater power,
quenched yet unquenched by the veil of the night.
So grows the soul of man ever upward,
quenched yet unquenched by the darkness of night.*

T2, V25.
*I, Death, come, and yet I remain not,
for life eternal exists in the ALL;
only an obstacle, I in the pathway,
quick to be conquered by the infinite light.
Awaken, O flame that burns ever inward,
flame forth and conquer the veil of the night."*

T2, V26.
Then in the midst of the flames in the darkness
grew there one that drove forth the night,
flaming, expanding, ever brighter,
until at last was nothing but Light.
Then spoke my guide, the voice of the master:
"See your own soul as it grows in the light,
free now forever from the Lord of the night."

T2, V27.
Forward he led me through many great spaces
filled with the mysteries of the Children of Light;
mysteries that man may never yet know of
until he, too, is a Sun of the Light.
Backward then HE led me
into the Light of the Hall of the Light.

Knelt I then before the great Masters,
Lords of ALL from the cycles above.

T2, V28.
Spoke HE then with words of great power saying:
*"Thou has been made free of the Halls of Amenti.
Choose thou thy work among the children of men."*

T2, V29.
Then spoke I:
*"O, great master, let me be a teacher of men,
leading them onward and upward
until they, too, are lights among men;
freed from the veil of the night
that surrounds them,
flaming with light
that shall shine among men."*

T2, V30.
Spoke to me then the voice:
*"Go, as ye will. So be it decreed.
Master are ye of your destiny,
free to take or reject at will.
Take ye the power,
take ye the wisdom.
Shine as a light
among the children of men."*

T2, V31.
Upward then, led me the Dweller.

Dwelt I again among children of men,
teaching and showing some of my wisdom;
Sun of the Light, a fire among men.

T2, V32.
Now again I tread the path downward,
seeking the light in the darkness of night.
Hold ye and keep ye, preserve my record,
guide shall it be to the children of men.

NOTES

Chapter Three

Emerald Tablet Three:
The Key of Wisdom

Tablet 3, Verse 1.
I, Thoth, the Atlantean,
give of my wisdom, give of my knowledge,
give of my power.
Freely I give to the children of men.
Give that they, too, might have wisdom
to shine through the world
from the veil of the night.
Wisdom is power and power is wisdom,
one with each other, perfecting the whole.

T3, V2.
Be thou not proud, O man, in thy wisdom.
Discourse with the ignorant as well as the wise.
If one comes to thee full of knowledge,
listen and heed, for wisdom is all.

Tablet Three

T3, V3.
Keep thou not silent when evil is spoken
for Truth like the sunlight shines above all.

T3, V4.
He who over-steppeth the Law shall be punished,
for only through Law comes the freedom of men.

> Commentary: Punished by consequences of wrongful actions...not by some angry God!

T3, V5.
Cause thou not fear, for fear is a bondage,
a fetter that binds the darkness to men.

T3, V6.
Follow thine heart during thy lifetime.
Do thou more than is commanded of thee.

T3, V7.
When thou hast gained riches,
follow thou thine heart,
for all these are of no avail if thine heart be weary.
Diminish thou not the time of following thine heart.
It is abhorred of the soul.

> Commentary: To Thoth it was evident that true happiness can only be found by following the heart. Let your heart guide you. You will not go astray.

T3, V8.
They that are guided go not astray,
but they that are lost cannot find a straight path.
If thou go among men, make for thyself, Love,
the beginning and end of the heart.

T3, V9.
If one cometh unto thee for council,
let him speak freely,
that the thing
for which he hath come to thee may be done.
If he hesitates to open his heart to thee,
it is because thou, the judge, doeth the wrong.

T3, V10.
Repeat thou not extravagant speech,
neither listen thou to it,
for it is the utterance of one not in equilibrium.
Speak thou not of it,
so that he before thee may know wisdom.

T3, V11.
Silence is of great profit.
An abundance of speech profiteth nothing.

T3, V12.
Exalt not thine heart above the children of men,
lest it be brought lower than the dust.

Tablet Three

T3, V13.
If thou be great among men,
be honored for knowledge and gentleness.

T3, V14.
If thou seeketh to know the nature of a friend,
ask not his companion,
but pass a time alone with him.
Debate with him,
testing his heart by his words and his bearing.

> Commentary: No need to listen to gossip to find the true measure of a friend. Spend time with him/her, talk with him/her, and their heart will reveal all to you.

T3, V15.
That which goeth into the store-house
must come forth,
and the things that are thine
must be shared with a friend.

T3, V16.
Knowledge is regarded by the fool as ignorance,
and the things that are profitable are to him hurtful.
He liveth in death.
It is therefore his food.

Tablet Three

T3, V17.
The wise man lets his heart overflow
but keeps silent his mouth.

T3, V18.
O men, list to the voice of wisdom;
list to the voice of light.
Mysteries there are in the Cosmos
that unveiled fill the world with their light.
Let he who would be free
from the bonds of darkness
first divine the material from the immaterial,
the fire from the earth;
for know ye that as earth descends to earth,
so also fire ascends unto fire
and becomes one with fire.
He who knows the fire that is within himself
shall ascend unto the eternal fire
and dwell in it eternally.

T3, V19.
Fire, the inner fire, is the most potent of all force,
for it overcometh all things
and penetrates to all things of the Earth.
Man supports himself only on that which resists.
So Earth must resist man else he existeth not.

Tablet Three

T3, V20.
All eyes do not see with the same vision,
for to one an object appears of one form and color
and to a different eye of another.
So also the infinite fire,
changing from color to color,
is never the same from day to day.

T3, V21.
Thus, speak I, THOTH, of my wisdom,
for man is a fire burning bright through the night;
never is quenched in the veil of the darkness,
never is quenched by the veil of the night.

T3, V22.
Into men's hearts, I looked by my wisdom,
found them not free from the bondage of strife.
Free from the toils, thy fire, O my brother,
lest it be buried in the shadow of night!

T3, V23.
Hark ye, O man, and list to this wisdom:
where do name and form cease?
Only in consciousness, invisible,
an infinite force of radiance bright.
The forms that ye create
by brightening thy vision
are truly effects that follow thy cause.

Tablet Three

T3, V24.
Man is a star bound to a body,
until in the end, he is freed through his strife.
Only by struggle and toiling thy utmost
shall the star within thee bloom out in new life.
He who knows the commencement of all things,
free is his star from the realms of night.

T3, V25.
Remember, O man, that all which exists
is only another form of that which exists not.
Everything that has being
is passing into yet other being
and thou thyself are not an exception.

T3, V26.
Consider the Law, for all is Law.
Seek not that which is not of the Law,
for such exists only in the illusions of the senses.

T3, V27.
Wisdom cometh to all her children
even as they cometh unto wisdom.

T3, V28.
All through the ages, the light has been hidden.
Awake, O man, and be wise.
Deep in the mysteries of life have I traveled,
seeking and searching for that which is hidden.
List ye, O man, and be wise.

T3, V29.
Far 'neath the earth crust, in the Halls of Amenti,
mysteries I saw that are hidden from men.
Oft have I journeyed the deep hidden passage,
looked on the Light that is Life among men.
There 'neath the flowers of Life ever living,
searched I the hearts and the secrets of men.
Found I that man is but living in darkness,
light of the great fire is hidden within.

T3, V30.
Before the Lords of hidden Amenti
learned I the wisdom I give unto men.
Masters are they of the great Secret Wisdom,
brought from the future of infinity's end.
Seven are they, the Lords of Amenti,
overlords they of the Children of Morning,
Suns of the cycles, Masters of Wisdom.
Formed are not they as the children of men?
THREE, FOUR, FIVE AND SIX, SEVEN, EIGHT, NINE
are the titles of the Masters of men.

T3, V31.
Far from the future, formless yet forming,
came they as teachers for the children of men.
Live they forever, yet not of the living,
bound not to life and yet free from death.
Rule they forever with infinite wisdom,
bound yet not bound to the dark Halls of Death.

Life they have in them, yet life that is not life,
free from all are the Lords of the ALL.

T3, V32.
Forth from them, came forth the Logos,
instruments they of the power o'er all.
Vast is their countenance,
yet hidden in smallness,
formed by a forming,
known yet unknown.

T3, V33.
THREE holds the key of all hidden magic,
creator he of the Halls of the Dead;
sending forth power, shrouding with darkness,
binding the souls of the children of men;
sending the darkness, binding the soul force;
director of negative to the children of men.

T3, V34.
FOUR is he who looses the power.
Lord, he, of Life to the children of men.
Light is his body, flame is his countenance;
freer of souls to the children of men.

T3, V35.
FIVE is the master, the Lord of all magic -
Key to The Word that resounds among men.

T3, V36.
SIX is the Lord of Light, the hidden pathway,
path of the souls of the children of men.

T3, V37.
SEVEN is he who is Lord of the vastness,
master of Space and the key of the Times.

T3, V38.
EIGHT is he who orders the progress;
weighs and balances the journey of men.

T3, V39.
NINE is the father, vast he of countenance,
forming and changing from out of the formless.

T3, V40.
Meditate on the symbols I give thee.
Keys are they, though hidden from men.

T3, V41.
Reach ever upward, O Soul of the morning.
Turn thy thoughts upward to Light and to Life.
Find in the keys of the numbers I bring thee,
light on the pathway from life unto life.

T3, V42.
Seek ye with wisdom. Turn thy thoughts inward.
Close not thy mind to the flower of Light.

T3, V43.
Place in thy body a thought-formed picture.
Think of the numbers that lead thee to Life.

T3, V44.
Clear is the pathway to he who has wisdom.
Open the door to the Kingdom of Light.

T3, V45.
Pour forth thy flame as a Sun of the morning.
Shut out the darkness and live in the day.

T3, V46.
Take thee, O man, as part of thy being,
the Seven who are but are not as they seem.
Opened, O man, have I my wisdom.
Follow the path in the way I have led.

T3, V47.
Masters of Wisdom,
SUN of the MORNING
LIGHT and LIFE to the children of men.

NOTES

Chapter Four

Emerald Tablet Four:
The Space Born

Tablet 4, Verse 1.
List ye, O man, to the voice of wisdom,
list to the voice of THOTH, the Atlantean.
Freely I give to thee of my wisdom,
gathered from the time and space of this cycle;
master of mysteries, SUN of the morning,
living forever, a child of the LIGHT,
shining with brightness, star of the morning,
THOTH the teacher of men, is of ALL.

T4, V2.
Long time ago, I, in my childhood,
lay 'neath the stars on long-buried ATLANTIS,
dreaming of mysteries far above men.
Then in my heart grew there a great longing
to conquer the pathway that led to the stars.

T4, V3.
Year after year, I sought after wisdom,

seeking new knowledge, following the way,
until at last my SOUL, in great travail,
broke from its bondage and bounded away.
Free was I from the bondage of earth-men.
Free from the body, I flashed through the night.
Unlocked at last for me was the star-space.
Free was I from the bondage of night.
Now to the end of space sought I wisdom,
far beyond knowledge of finite man.

T4, V4.
Far into space, my SOUL traveled freely
into infinity's circle of light.
Strange, beyond knowledge,
were some of the planets,
great and gigantic, beyond dreams of men.
Yet found I Law, in all of its beauty,
working through and among them
as here among men.
Flashed forth my soul through infinity's beauty,
far through space I flew with my thoughts.

T4, V5.
Rested I there on a planet of beauty.
Strains of harmony filled all the air.
Shapes there were, moving in Order,
great and majestic as stars in the night;
mounting in harmony, ordered equilibrium,
symbols of the Cosmic, like unto Law.

T4, V6.
Many the stars I passed in my journey,
many the races of men on their worlds;
some reaching high as stars of the morning,
some falling low in the blackness of night.
Each and all of them struggling upward,
gaining the heights and plumbing the depths,
moving at times in realms of brightness,
living through darkness, gaining the Light.

T4, V7.
Know, O man, that Light is thine heritage.
Know that darkness is only a veil.
Sealed in thine heart is brightness eternal,
waiting the moment of freedom to conquer,
waiting to rend the veil of the night.

T4, V8.
Some I found who had conquered the ether.
Free of space were they while yet they were men.
Using the force that is the foundation of ALL things,
far in space constructed they a planet,
drawn by the force that flows through the ALL;
condensing, coalescing the ether
into forms that grew as they willed.
Outstripping in science, they, all of the races,
mighty in wisdom, sons of the stars.

T4, V9.
Long time I paused, watching their wisdom.

Saw them create from out of the ether
cities gigantic of rose and gold.
Formed forth from the primal element,
base of all matter, the ether far flung.

T4, V10.
Far in the past, they had conquered the ether,
freed themselves from the bondage of toil;
formed in their mind only a picture
and swiftly created, it grew.

T4, V11.
Forth then, my soul sped, throughout the Cosmos,
seeing ever, new things and old;
learning that man is truly space-born,
a Sun of the Sun, a child of the stars.

T4, V12.
Know ye, O man, whatever form ye inhabit,
surely it is one with the stars.
Thy bodies are nothing but planets
revolving around their central suns.
When ye have gained the light of all wisdom,
free shall ye be to shine in the ether -
one of the Suns that light outer darkness -
one of the space-born grown into Light.
Just as the stars in time lose their brilliance,
light passing from them into the great source,
so, O man, thy soul passes onward,
leaving behind the darkness of night.

T4, V13.
Formed forth ye, from the primal ether,
filled with the brilliance that flows from the source,
bound by the ether coalesced around,
yet ever it flames until at last it is free.
Lift up your flame from out of the darkness,
fly from the night and ye shall be free.

T4, V14.
Traveled I through the space-time,
knowing my soul at last was set free,
knowing that now might I pursue wisdom.
Until at last, I passed to a plane,
hidden from knowledge,
known not to wisdom,
extension beyond all that we know.
Now, O man, when I had this knowing,
happy my soul grew, for now I was free.
Listen, ye space-born, list to my wisdom:
know ye not that ye, too, will be free.

T4, V15.
List ye again, O man, to my wisdom,
that hearing, ye too, might live and be free.
Not of the earth are ye - earthy,
but child of the Infinite Cosmic Light.

T4, V16.
Know ye not, O man, of your heritage?
Know ye not ye are truly the Light?

Sun of the Great Sun, when ye gain wisdom,
truly aware of your kinship with Light.

T4, V17.
Now, to ye, I give knowledge,
freedom to walk in the path I have trod,
showing ye truly how by my striving,
I trod the path that leads to the stars.

T4, V18.
Hark ye, O man, and know of thy bondage,
know how to free thyself from the toils.
Out of the darkness shall ye rise upward,
one with the Light and one with the stars.
Follow ye ever the path of wisdom.
Only by this can ye rise from below.
Ever man's destiny leads him onward
into the Curves of Infinity's ALL.

T4, V19.
Know ye, O man, that all space is ordered.
Only by Order are ye One with the ALL.
Order and balance are the Law of the Cosmos.
Follow and ye shall be One with the ALL.

T4, V20.
He who would follow the pathway of wisdom,
open must be to the flower of life,
extending his consciousness out of the darkness,
flowing through time and space in the ALL.

*Deep in the silence, first ye must linger
until at last ye are free from desire,
free from the longing to speak in the silence.
Conquer by silence, the bondage of words.
Abstaining from eating
until we have conquered desire for food,
that is bondage of soul.*

T4, V21.
*Then lie ye down in the darkness.
Close ye your eyes from the rays of the Light.*

*Center thy soul-force
in the place of thine consciousness,
shaking it free from the bonds of the night.
Place in thy mind-place the image thou desireth.
Picture the place thou desireth to see.
Vibrate back and forth with thy power.
Loosen the soul from out of its night.
Fiercely must thou shake with all of thy power
until at last thy soul shall be free.*

T4, V22.
*Mighty beyond words is the flame of the Cosmic,
hanging in planes, unknown to man;
mighty and balanced, moving in Order,
music of harmonies, far beyond man.
Speaking with music, singing with color,
flame from the beginning of Eternity's ALL.*

T4, V23.
Spark of the flame art thou, O my children,
burning with color and living with music.
List to the voice and thou shalt be free.

T4, V24.
Consciousness free is fused with the Cosmic,
One with the Order and Law of the ALL.

T4, V25.
Knew ye not man, that out of the darkness,
Light shall flame forth, a symbol of ALL.

T4, V26.
Pray ye this prayer for attaining of wisdom.
Pray for the coming of Light to the ALL:

*"Mighty SPIRIT of LIGHT
that shines through the Cosmos,
draw my flame closer in harmony to thee.
Lift up my fire from out of the darkness,
magnet of fire that is One with the ALL.
Lift up my soul, thou mighty and potent.
Child of the Light, turn not away.
Draw me in power to melt in thy furnace;
One with all things and all things in One,
fire of the life-strain and One with the Brain."*

T4, V27.
When ye have freed thy soul from its bondage,
know that for ye the darkness is gone.
Ever through space ye may seek wisdom,
bound not by fetters forged in the flesh.

T4, V28.
Onward and upward into the morning,
free flash, O Soul, to the realms of Light.
Move thou in Order, move thou in Harmony,
freely shalt move with the Children of Light.

T4, V29.
Seek ye and know ye, my KEY of Wisdom.
Thus, O man, ye shall surely be free.

NOTES

Chapter Five

Emerald Tablet Five:
The Dweller of Unal

Tablet 5, Verse 1.
Oft dream I of buried Atlantis,
lost in the ages that have passed into night.
Aeon on aeon thou existed in beauty,
a light shining through the darkness of night.

T5, V2.
Mighty in power, ruling the earth-born,
Lord of the Earth in Atlantis' day.
King of the nations, master of wisdom,
LIGHT through SUNTAL, Keeper of the way,
dwelt in his TEMPLE, the MASTER of UNAL,
LIGHT of the Earth in Atlantis' day.

T5, V3.
Master, HE, from a cycle beyond us,
living in bodies as one among men.
Not as the earth-born, HE from beyond us,
SUN of a cycle, advanced beyond men.

Tablet Five

T5, V4.
Know ye, O man, that HORLET the Master,
was never one with the children of men.
Far in the past time
when Atlantis first grew as a power,
appeared there one with the KEY of WISDOM,
showing the way of LIGHT to all.

T5, V5.
Showed he to all men the path of attainment,
way of the Light that flows among men.
Mastering darkness, leading the MAN-SOUL,
upward to heights that were One with the Light.

T5, V6.
Divided the Kingdoms, HE into sections.
Ten were they, ruled by children of men.
Upon another, built HE a TEMPLE,
built but not by the children of men.

T5, V7.
Out of the ETHER called HE its substance,
molded and formed by the power of YTOLAN
into the forms HE built with His mind.
Mile upon mile it covered the island,
space upon space it grew in its might.
Black, yet not black, but dark like the space-time,
deep in its heart the ESSENCE of LIGHT.
Swiftly the TEMPLE grew into being,

molded and shaped by the WORD of the DWELLER,
called from the formless into a form.

T5, V8.
Built HE then, within it, great chambers,
filled them with forms called forth from the ETHER,
filled them with wisdom called forth by His mind.

T5, V9.
Formless was HE within his TEMPLE,
yet was HE formed in the image of men.
Dwelling among them, yet not of them,
strange and far different was HE
from the children of men.

T5, V10.
Chose HE then from among the people,
THREE who became his gateway.
Chose HE the THREE from the Highest
to become his links with Atlantis.
Messengers they, who carried his council,
to the kings of the children of men.

T5, V11.
Brought HE forth others and taught them wisdom;
teachers, they, to the children of men.
Placed HE them on the island of UNDAL
to stand as teachers of LIGHT to men.

T5, V12.
Each of those who were thus chosen,
taught must he be for years five and ten.
Only thus could he have understanding
to bring LIGHT to the children of men.
Thus there came into being the Temple,
a dwelling place for the Master of men.

T5, V13.
I, THOTH, have ever sought wisdom,
searching in darkness and searching in Light.
Long in my youth I traveled the pathway,
seeking ever new knowledge to gain.
Until after much striving,
one of the THREE, to me brought the LIGHT.
Brought HE to me the commands of the DWELLER,
called me from darkness into the LIGHT.
Brought HE me, before the DWELLER,
deep in the Temple before the great FIRE.

T5, V14.
There on the great throne, beheld I, the DWELLER,
clothed with the LIGHT and flashing with fire.
Down I knelt before that great wisdom,
feeling the LIGHT flowing through me in waves.
Heard I then the voice of the DWELLER:

"O darkness, come into the Light.
Long have ye sought the pathway to LIGHT.
Each soul on earth that loosens its fetters,

*shall soon be made free from the bondage of night.
Forth from the darkness have ye arisen,
closer approached the Light of your goal.
Here ye shall dwell as one of my children,
keeper of records gathered by wisdom,
instrument thou of the LIGHT from beyond.
Ready be thou made to do what is needed,
preserver of wisdom through the ages of darkness,
that shall come fast on the children of men.
Live thee here and drink of all wisdom.
Secrets and mysteries unto thee shall unveil."*

T5, V15.
Then answered I, the MASTER OF CYCLES, saying:
*"O Light, that descended to men,
give thou to me of thy wisdom
that I might be a teacher of men.
Give thou of thy LIGHT that I may be free."*

T5, V16.
Spoke then to me again, the MASTER:
*"Age after age shall ye live through your wisdom,
Aye, when o'er Atlantis the ocean waves roll,
holding the Light, though hidden in darkness,
ready to come when e'er thou shalt call.
Go thee now and learn greater wisdom.
Grow thou through LIGHT to Infinity's ALL."*

T5, V17.
Long then dwelt I in the Temple of the DWELLER

until at last I was One with the LIGHT.

Followed I then the path to the star planes,
followed I then the pathway to LIGHT.
Deep into Earth's heart I followed the pathway,
learning the secrets, below as above;
learning the pathway to the HALLS of AMENTI;
learning the LAW that balances the world.
To Earth's hidden chambers
pierced I by my wisdom,
deep through the Earth's crust, into the pathway,
hidden for ages from the children of men.
Unveiled before me, ever more wisdom
until I reached a new knowledge:
found that all is part of an ALL,
great and yet greater than all that we know.
Searched I Infinity's heart through all the ages.
Deep and yet deeper, more mysteries I found.

T5, V18.
Now, as I look back through the ages,
know I that wisdom is boundless,
ever grown greater throughout the ages,
One with Infinity's greater than all.

T5, V19.
Light there was in ancient ATLANTIS.
Yet, darkness, too, was hidden in all.
Fell from the Light into the darkness,

some who had risen to heights among men.
Proud they became because of their knowledge,
proud were they of their place among men.
Deep delved they into the forbidden,
opened the gateway that led to below.
Sought they to gain ever more knowledge
but seeking to bring it up from below.

T5, V20.
He who descends below must have balance,
else he is bound by lack of our Light.
Opened, they then, by their knowledge,
pathways forbidden to man.

T5, V21.
But, in His Temple, all-seeing, the DWELLER,
lay in his AGWANTI,
while through Atlantis, His soul roamed free.
Saw HE the Atlanteans, by their magic,
opening the gateway
that would bring to Earth a great woe.
Fast fled His soul then, back to His body.
Up HE arose from His AGWANTI.
Called HE the Three mighty messengers.
Gave the commands that shattered the world.

T5, V22.
Deep 'neath Earth's crust to the HALLS of AMENTI,
swiftly descended the DWELLER.

Called HE then on the powers
the Seven Lords wielded;
changed the Earth's balance.
Down sank Atlantis beneath the dark waves.

T5, V23.
Shattered the gateway that had been opened;
shattered the doorway that led down below.
All of the islands were shattered except UNAL,
and part of the island of the sons of the DWELLER.
Preserved HE them to be the teachers,
Lights on the path for those to come after,
Lights for the lesser children of men.

T5, V24.
Called HE then, I THOTH, before him,
gave me commands for all I should do, saying;
"Take thou, O THOTH, all of your wisdom.
Take all your records, Take all your magic.
Go thou forth as a teacher of men.
Go thou forth preserving the records
until in time LIGHT grows among men.
LIGHT shalt thou be all through the ages,
hidden yet found by enlightened men.
Over all Earth, give WE ye power,
free thou to give or to take it away.
Gather thou now the sons of Atlantis.
Take them and flee to the people of the rock caves.
Fly to the land of the Children of KHEM."

T5, V25.
Then gathered I the sons of Atlantis.
Into the spaceship I brought all my records,
brought the records of sunken Atlantis.
Gathered I all of my powers,
instruments many of mighty magic.

T5, V26.
Up then we rose on wings of the morning.
High we arose above the Temple,
leaving behind the Three and DWELLER,
deep in the HALLS 'neath the Temple.
Down 'neath the waves sank the great Temple,
closing the pathway to the LORDS of the Cycles.
Yet ever to him who has knowing,
open shall be the path to AMENTI.

T5, V27.
Fast fled we then on the wings of the morning,
fled to the land of the children of KHEM.
There by my power,
I conquered and ruled them.
Raised I to LIGHT, the children of KHEM.

T5, V28.
Deep 'neath the rocks, I buried my spaceship,
waiting the time when man might be free.
Over the spaceship, erected a marker
in the form of a lion yet like unto man.

Tablet Five

There 'neath the image rests yet my spaceship,
forth to be brought when need shall arise.

> Commentary: I believe this is referring to the Sphinx.

T5, V29.
Know ye, O man, that far in the future,
invaders shall come from out of the deep.
Then awake, ye who have wisdom.
Bring forth my ship and conquer with ease.

T5, V30.
Deep 'neath the image lies my secret.
Search and find in the pyramid I built.
Each to the other is the Keystone;
each the gateway that leads into LIFE.
Follow the KEY I leave behind me.
Seek and the doorway to LIFE shall be thine.
Seek thou in my pyramid,
deep in the passage that ends in a wall.
Use thou the KEY of the SEVEN,
and open to thee the pathway will fall.

T5, V31.
Now unto thee I have given my wisdom.
Now unto thee I have given my way.
Follow the pathway. Solve thou my secrets.
Unto thee I have shown the way.

NOTES

Chapter Six

Emerald Tablet Six:
The Key of Magic

Tablet 6, Verse 1.
Hark ye, O man, to the wisdom of magic.
Hark to the knowledge of powers forgotten.
Long, long ago in the days of the first man,
warfare began between darkness and light.
Men, then as now,
were filled with both darkness and light;
and while in some, darkness held sway,
in others, light filled the soul.

T6, V2.
Aye, age old is this warfare,
the eternal struggle between darkness and light.
Fiercely is it fought all through the ages,
using strange powers hidden to man.

T6, V3.
Adepts have there been, filled with the blackness,
struggling always against the light;

but others there are who, filled with brightness,
have ever conquered the darkness of night.
Where e'er ye may be in all ages and planes,
surely ye shall know of the battle with night.
Long ages ago, the SUNS of the Morning,
descending, found the world filled with night.
There in that past time began the struggle,
the age old battle of darkness and Light.

T6, V4.
Many in that time were so filled with darkness
that only feebly flamed the light from the night.

> *Note from Rebecca: This is in line with something Sanat Kumara told me long ago: "At one time the flame in man's heart was almost extinguished. It was then I intervened for the souls of all men".

T6, V5.
Some there were, masters of darkness,
who sought to fill all with their darkness;
sought to draw others into their night.
Fiercely withstood they, the masters of brightness:
fiercely fought they from the darkness of night.
Sought they ever to tighten the fetters,
the chains that bind man to the darkness of night.
Used they always the dark magic,
brought into man by the power of darkness;
magic that enshrouded man's soul with darkness.

T6, V6.
Banded together in an order,
BROTHERS of DARKNESS,
they through the ages,
antagonists they to the children of men.
Walked they always secret and hidden,
found, yet not found, by the children of men.
Forever they walked and worked in darkness,
hiding from the light in the darkness of night.
Silently, secretly, use they their power,
enslaving and binding the souls of men.

T6, V7.
Unseen they come, and unseen they go.
Man, in his ignorance, calls THEM from below.

T6, V8.
Dark is the way the DARK BROTHERS travel,
dark with a darkness not of the night,
traveling o'er Earth
they walk through man's dreams.
Power have they gained
from the darkness around them
to call other dwellers from out of their plane,
in ways that are dark and unseen by man.
Into man's mind-space reach the DARK BROTHERS.
Around it, they close the veil of their night.
There through its lifetime
that soul dwells in bondage,
bound by the fetters of the VEIL of the night.

Mighty are they in the forbidden knowledge,
forbidden because it is one with the night.

T6, V9.
Hark ye, O man, and list to my warning:
be ye free from the bondage of night.
Surrender not your soul
to the BROTHERS OF DARKNESS.
Keep thy face ever turned toward the LIGHT.
Know ye not, O man, that your sorrow,
only has come through the Veil of the night.
Aye, man, heed ye my warning:
strive ever upward,
turn your soul toward the LIGHT.

T6, V10.
The BROTHERS of DARKNESS seek for their brothers
those who have traveled the pathway of LIGHT.
For well know they that those who have traveled
far towards the Sun in their pathway of LIGHT
have great and yet greater power
to bind with darkness the children of LIGHT.

T6, V11.
List ye, O man, to he who comes to you.
But weigh in the balance if his words be of LIGHT.
For many there are who walk in DARK BRIGHTNESS
and yet are not the children of LIGHT.

T6, V12.
Easy it is to follow their pathway,
easy to follow the path that they lead.
But yet, O man, heed ye my warning:
Light comes only to him who strives.
Hard is the pathway that leads to the WISDOM,
hard is the pathway that leads to the LIGHT.
Many shall ye find, the stones in your pathway;
many the mountains to climb toward the LIGHT.
Yet know ye, O man, to him that o'ercometh,
free will he be of the pathway of Light.
Follow ye not the DARK BROTHERS ever.
Always be ye a child of the Light.
For know ye, O man,
in the end LIGHT must conquer
and darkness and night be banished from Light.

T6, V13.
Listen, O man, and heed ye this wisdom;
even as darkness, so is the LIGHT.
When darkness is banished and all Veils are rended,
out there shall flash from the darkness, the LIGHT.

T6, V14.
Even as exist among men the DARK BROTHERS,
so there exist the BROTHERS of LIGHT.
Antagonists they of the BROTHERS of DARKNESS,
seeking to free men from the night.
Powers have they, mighty and potent.

Knowing the LAW, the planets obey.
Work they ever in harmony and order,
freeing the man-soul from its bondage of night.
Secret and hidden, walk they also.
Known not are they to the children of men.
Yet know that ever they walk with thee,
Showing the WAY to the children of men.

T6, V15.
Ever have THEY fought the DARK BROTHERS,
conquered and conquering time without end.
Yet always LIGHT shall in the end be master,
driving away the darkness of night.

Aye, man, know ye this knowing:
always beside thee walk the Children of Light.

T6, V16.
Masters they of the SUN power,
ever unseen yet the guardians of men.
Open to all is their pathway,
open to he who will walk in the LIGHT.
Free are THEY of DARK AMENTI,
free of the HALLS, where LIFE reigns supreme.
SUNS are they and LORDS of the morning,
Children of Light to shine among men.
Like man are they and yet are unlike,
Never divided were they in the past.
ONE have they been in ONENESS eternal,
throughout all space since the beginning of time.

Up did they come in Oneness with the ALL ONE,
up from the first-space, formed and unformed.

T6, V17.
Given to man have they secrets
that shall guard and protect him from all harm.
He who would travel the path of a master,
free must he be from the bondage of night.

T6, V18.
Conquer must he the formless and shapeless,
conquer must he the phantom of fear.
Knowing, must he gain of all of the secrets,
travel the pathway that leads through the darkness,
yet ever before him keep the light of his goal.
Obstacles great shall he meet in the pathway,
yet press on to the LIGHT of the SUN.

T6, V19.
Hear ye, O man, the SUN is the symbol
of the LIGHT that shines at the end of thy road.
Now to thee give I the secrets:
now to meet the dark power,
meet and conquer the fear from the night.
Only by knowing can ye conquer,
Only by knowing can ye have LIGHT.

T6, V20.
Now I give unto thee the knowledge,
known to the MASTERS,

the knowing that conquers all the dark fears.
Use this, the wisdom I give thee.
MASTERS thou shalt be of the BROTHERS of NIGHT.

T6, V21.
When unto thee there comes a feeling,
drawing thee nearer to the dark gate,
examine thine heart and find if the feeling
thou hast has come from within.
If thou shalt find the darkness thine own thoughts,
banish them forth from the place in thy mind.
Send through thy body a wave of vibration,
irregular first and regular second,
repeating time after time until free.
Start the WAVE FORCE in thy BRAIN CENTER.
Direct it in waves from thine head to thy foot.

T6, V22,
But if thou findest thine heart is not darkened,
be sure that a force is directed to thee.
Only by knowing can thou overcome it.
Only by wisdom can thou hope to be free.
Knowledge brings wisdom and wisdom is power.
Attain and ye shall have power o'er all.

T6, V23.
Seek ye first a place bound with darkness.
Place ye a circle around about thee.
Stand erect in the midst of the circle.
Use thou this formula, and thou shalt be free.

*Raise thou thine hands to the dark space above thee.
Close thou thine eyes and draw in the LIGHT.
Call to the SPIRIT OF LIGHT through the Space-Time,
using these words and thou shalt be free:
"Fill thou my body, O SPIRIT OF LIFE,
fill thou my body with SPIRIT OF LIGHT.
Come from the FLOWER
that shines through the darkness.
Come from the HALLS where the Seven Lords rule.
Name them by name, I, the Seven:
THREE, FOUR, FIVE,
and SIX, SEVEN, EIGHT-NINE.*

T6, V24.
*By their names I call them to aid me,
free me and save me from the darkness of night:
UNTANAS, QUERTAS, CHIETAL,
and GOYANA, HUERTAL, SEMVETA-ARDAL.
By their names I implore thee,
free me from darkness
and fill me with LIGHT."*

T6, V25.
*Know ye, O man, that when ye have done this,
ye shall be free from the fetters that bind ye,
cast off the bondage of the BROTHERS of NIGHT.
See ye not that the names have the power
to free by vibration the fetters that bind?
Use them at need to free thou thine brother
so that he, too, may come forth from the night.*

T6, V26.
Thou, O man, art thy brother's helper.
Let him not lie in the bondage of night.

T6, V27.
Now unto thee, give I my magic.
Take it and dwell on the pathway of LIGHT.

T6, V28.
LIGHT unto thee, LIFE unto thee,
SUN may thou be on the cycle above.

NOTES

Chapter Seven

Emerald Tablet Seven:
The Seven Lords

Tablet 7, Verse 1.
Hark ye, O man, and list to my Voice.
Open thy mind-space and drink of my wisdom.
Dark is the pathway of LIFE that ye travel.
Many the pitfalls that lie in thy way.
Seek ye ever to gain greater wisdom.
Attain and it shall be light on thy way.

T7, V2.
Open thy SOUL, O man, to the Cosmic
and let it flow in as one with thy SOUL.
LIGHT is eternal and darkness is fleeting.
Seek ye ever, O man, for the LIGHT.
Know ye that ever as Light fills thy being,
darkness for thee shall soon disappear.

T7, V3.
Open thy soul to the BROTHERS of BRIGHTNESS.
Let them enter and fill thee with LIGHT.

Lift up thine eyes to the LIGHT of the Cosmos.
Keep thou ever thy face to the goal.
Only by gaining the light of all wisdom,
art thou one with the Infinite goal.
Seek ye ever the Oneness eternal.
Seek ye ever the Light of the goal.

T7, V4.
Light is infinite and Light is finite,
separate only by darkness in man.
Seek ye to rend the Veil of the Darkness.
Bring thou together the Light into One.

T7, V5.
Hear ye, O man, list to my Voice
singing the song of Light and of Life.
Throughout all space, Light is prevalent,
encompassing ALL with its banners of flame.
Seek ye forever in the Veil of the Darkness,
somewhere ye shall surely find Light.
Hidden and buried, lost to man's knowledge,
deep in the finite, the Infinite exists.
Lost, but existing,
flowing through all things,
living in ALL is the INFINITE BRAIN.

T7, V6.
In all space, there is only ONE wisdom.
Though seeming decided, it is ONE in the ONE.

All that exists comes forth from the LIGHT,
and the LIGHT comes forth from the ALL.

T7, V7.
Everything created is based upon ORDER:
LAW rules the space where the INFINITE dwells.
Forth from equilibrium came the great cycles,
moving in harmony toward Infinity's end.

T7, V8.
Know ye, O man, that far in the space-time,
INFINITY itself shall pass into change.
Hear ye and list to the Voice of Wisdom:
Know that ALL is of ALL evermore.
Know that through time thou may pursue wisdom
and find ever more light on the way.
Aye, thou shalt find that ever receding,
thy goal shall elude thee from day unto day.

T7, V9.
Long time ago, in the HALLS OF AMENTI,
I, Thoth, stood before the LORDS of the cycles.
Mighty, THEY in their aspects of power;
mighty, THEY in the wisdom unveiled.

T7, V10.
Led by the Dweller, first did I see them.
But afterwards free was I of their presence,
free to enter their conclave at will.

Oft did I journey down the dark pathway
unto the HALL where the LIGHT ever glows.

T7, V11.
Learned I of the Masters of cycles,
wisdom brought from the cycles above us,
knowledge brought from INFINITY'S ALL.
Many the questions I asked
of the LORDS of the cycles.
Great was the wisdom they gave unto me.
Now unto thee I give of this wisdom,
drawn from the Flame of Infinity's fire.

T7, V12.
Deep in the DARK HALLS sit the SEVEN,
units of consciousness from cycles above.
Manifest THEY in this cycle
as guides of man to the knowledge of ALL.
Seven are they, mighty in power,
speaking these words through me to men.
Time after time, stood I before them
listening to words that came not with sound.

T7, V13.
Once said THEY unto me:
"O man, wouldst thou gain wisdom?
Seek for it in the heart of the flame.
Wouldst thou gain knowledge of power?
Seek ye it in the heart of the flame.

*Wouldst be one with the heart of the flame?
Seek then within thine own hidden flame."*

T7, V14.
Many the times spoke THEY to me,
teaching me wisdom not of the world;
showing me ever new paths to brightness;
teaching me wisdom brought from above.
Giving knowledge of operation,
learning of LAW, the order of ALL.

T7, V15.
Spoke to me again, the Seven, saying:
*"From far beyond time are WE come, O man.
Traveled WE from beyond the SPACE-TIME,
aye, from the place of Infinity's end.
When ye and all of thy brethren were formless,
formed forth were WE from the order of ALL.
Not as men are WE,
though once WE, too, were as men.
Out of the Great Void were WE formed forth
in order and by LAW.
For know ye that that which is formed
truly is formless, having form only to thine eyes."*

T7, V16.
And again, unto me spoke the Seven, saying:
*"Child of the LIGHT, O THOTH, art thou,
free to travel the bright path upward
until at the last ALL ONES become ONE.*

T7, V17.
Forth were WE formed after our order:
THREE, FOUR, FIVE, and SIX, SEVEN, EIGHT-NINE.
Know ye that these are the number of cycles
that WE descend from unto man.
Each having here a duty to fulfill;
each having here a force to control.
Yet are we ONE with the SOUL of our cycle.
Yet are WE, too, seeking a goal.

T7, V18.
Far beyond man's conception,
Infinity extends into a greater than ALL.
There, in a time that is yet not a time,
we shall ALL become ONE
with a greater than ALL.
Time and space are moving in circles.
Know ye their law, and ye, too, shall be free.
Aye, free shall ye be to move through the cycles-
pass the guardians that dwell at the door."

T7, V19.
Then to me spoke HE of NINE, saying:
"Aeons and aeons have I existed,
knowing not LIFE and tasting not death.
For know ye, O man, that far in the future,
life and death shall be one with the ALL.
Each so perfected by balancing the other
that neither exists in the Oneness of ALL.

*In men of this cycle, the life force is rampant,
but life in its growth becomes one with the ALL.
Here, I manifest in this your cycle,
but yet am I there in your future of time.*

*T7, V20.
Yet to me, time exists not,
for in my world time exists not,
for formless are WE.*

*Life have WE not, but yet have existence,
fuller and greater and freer than thee.*

*T7, V21.
Man is a flame bound to a mountain,
but WE in our cycle shall ever be free.
Know ye, O man, that when ye have progressed
into the cycles that lengthen above,
life itself will pass to the darkness
and only the essence of Soul shall remain."*

*T7, V22.
Then to me spoke the LORD of the EIGHT saying:
"All that ye know is but part of little.
Not as yet have ye touched on the Great.
Far out in space where LIGHT reigns supreme,
came I into the LIGHT.
Formed was I also but not as ye are.*

Tablet Seven

T7, V23.
*Body of Light was my formless form formed.
Know I not LIFE and know I not DEATH,
yet master am I of all that exists.
Seek ye to find the path through the barriers.
Travel the road that leads to the LIGHT."*

T7, V24.
*Spoke again to me the NINE saying:
"Seek ye to find the path to beyond.
Not impossible is it to grow
to a consciousness above.
For when TWO have become ONE
and ONE has become the ALL,
know ye the barrier has lifted,
and ye are made free of the road."
Grow thou from form to the formless.
Free may thou be of the road."*

T7, V25.
*Thus, through ages I listened,
learning the way to the ALL.
Now lift I my thoughts to the ALL-THING.
List ye and hear when it calls.*

T7, V26.
*"O LIGHT, all pervading,
One with ALL and ALL with ONE,
flow thou to me through the channel.
Enter thou so that I may be free.*

*Make me One with the ALL-SOUL,
shining from the blackness of night.
Free let me be of all space-time,
free from the Veil of the night.
I, a child of the LIGHT, command:
Free from the darkness to be."*

T7, V27.
Formless am I to the Light-Soul,
formless yet shining with Light.
Know I the bonds of the darkness
must shatter and fall before Light.

T7, V28.
Now give I this wisdom.
Free may ye be, O man,
living in light and in brightness.
Turn not thy face from the Light.
Thy soul dwells in realms of brightness.
Ye are a child of the Light.

T7, V29.
Turn thy thoughts inward not outward.
Find thou the Light-Soul within.
Know that thou art the MASTER.
All else is brought from within.
Grow thou to realms of brightness.
Hold thou thy thought on the Light.
Know thou art one with the Cosmos,
a flame and a Child of the Light.

T7, V30.
Now to thee gave I warning:
Let not thy thought turn away.
Know that the brightness
flows through thy body for aye.
Turn not to the DARK-BRIGHTNESS
that comes from the BROTHERS OF BLACK.
But keep thine eyes ever lifted,
thy soul in tune with the Light.

T7, V31.
Take ye this wisdom and heed it.
List to my Voice and obey.
Follow the pathway to brightness,
and thou shall be ONE with the way.

NOTES

Chapter Eight

Emerald Tablet Eight:
The Key of Mysteries

Tablet 8, Verse 1.
Unto thee, O man,
have I given my knowledge.
Unto thee have I given of Light.
Hear ye now and receive my wisdom
brought from space planes above and beyond.

T8, V2.
Not as man am I
for free have I become of dimensions and planes.
In each, take I on a new body.
In each, I change in my form.
Know I now that the formless is all there is of form.

T8, V3.
Great is the wisdom of the Seven.
Mighty are THEY from beyond.

Manifest THEY through their power,
filled by force from beyond.

T8, V4.
Hear ye these words of wisdom.
Hear ye and make them thine own.
Find in them the formless.
Find ye the key to beyond.
Mystery is but hidden knowledge.
Know and ye shall unveil.
Find the deep buried wisdom
and be master of darkness and Light.

T8, V5.
Deep are the mysteries around thee,
hidden the secrets of Old.
Search through the KEYS of my WISDOM.
Surely shall ye find the way
The gateway to power is secret,
but he who attains shall receive.
Look to the LIGHT! O my brother.
Open and ye shall receive.
Press on through the valley of darkness.
Overcome the dweller of night.
Keep ever thine eyes to the LIGHT-PLANE,
and thou shalt be One with the LIGHT.

T8, V6.
Man is in process of changing
to forms that are not of this world.

Grows he in time to the formless,
a plane on the cycle above.
Know ye, ye must become formless
before ye are one with the LIGHT.
List ye, O man, to my voice,
telling of pathways to Light,
showing the way of attainment
when ye shall be One with the Light.

T8, V7.
Search ye the mysteries of Earth's heart.
Learn of the LAW that exists,
holding the stars in their balance
by the force of the primordial mist.

T8, V8.
Seek ye the flame of the EARTH'S LIFE.
Bathe in the glare of its flame.
Follow the three-cornered pathway
until thou, too, art a flame.

T8, V9.
Speak thou in words without voice
to those who dwell down below.
Enter the blue-litten temple
and bathe in the fire of all life.

T8, V10.
Know, O man, thou art complex,
a being of earth and of fire.

Tablet Eight

Let thy flame shine out brightly.
Be thou only the fire.

T8, V11.
Wisdom is hidden in darkness.
When lit by the flame of the Soul,
find thou the wisdom and be LIGHT-BORN,
a Sun of the Light without form.
Seek thee ever more wisdom.
Find it in the heart of the flame.
Know that only by striving
can Light pour into thy brain.
Now have I spoken with wisdom.
List to my Voice and obey.
Tear open the Veils of the darkness.
Shine a LIGHT on the WAY.

T8, V12.
Speak I of Ancient Atlantis,
speak of the days
of the Kingdom of Shadows,
speak of the coming
of the children of shadows.
Out of the great deep were they called
by the wisdom of earth-men,
called for the purpose of gaining great power.

T8, V13.
Far in the past before Atlantis existed,

men there were who delved into darkness,
using dark magic, calling up beings
from the great deep below us.
Forth came they into this cycle.
Formless were they of another vibration,
existing unseen by the children of earth-men.
Only through blood could they have formed being.
Only through man could they live in the world.

T8, V14.
In ages past were they conquered by the Masters,
driven below to the place whence they came.
But some there were who remained,
hidden in spaces and planes unknown to man.
Lived they in Atlantis as shadows,
but at times they appeared among men.
Aye, when the blood was offered,
forth came they to dwell among men.

T8, V15.
In the form of man they moved amongst us,
but only to sight were they as are men.
Serpent-headed when the glamour was lifted
but appearing to man as men among men.
Crept they into the Councils,
taking forms that were like unto men.
Slaying by their arts
the chiefs of the kingdoms,
taking their form and ruling o'er man.

T8, V16.
Only by magic could they be discovered.
Only by sound could their faces be seen.
Sought they from the kingdom of shadows
to destroy man and rule in his place.

T8, V17.
But, know ye, the Masters were mighty in magic,
able to lift the Veil from the face of the serpent,
able to send him back to his place.
Came they to man and taught him the secret,
the WORD that only a man can pronounce.
Swift then they lifted the Veil from the serpent
and cast him forth from place among men.

T8, V18.
Yet, beware, the serpent still liveth
in a place that is open at times to the world.
Unseen they walk among thee
in places where the rites have been said.
Again as time passes onward
shall they take the semblance of men.

T8, V19.
Called may they be by the master
who knows the white or the black,
but only the white master may control
and bind them while in the flesh.

T8, V20.
Seek not the kingdom of shadows,
for evil will surely appear.
For only the master of brightness
shall conquer the shadow of fear.

T8, V21.
Know ye, O my brother,
that fear is an obstacle great.
Be master of all in the brightness,
the shadow will soon disappear.
Hear ye and heed my wisdom,
the voice of LIGHT is clear.
Seek not the valley of shadow,
and LIGHT only will appear.

> Comment: Turn your thoughts away from fearing the darkness. Embrace Light, chant Light . . . for the sound of your voice will dispel the dark.

T8, V22.
List ye, O man,
to the depth of my wisdom.
Speak I of knowledge hidden from man.
Far have I been
on my journey through SPACE-TIME,
even to the end of the space of this cycle.
Found I there the great barrier,
holding man from leaving this cycle.

Tablet Eight

Aye, glimpsed the HOUNDS of the Barrier,
lying in wait for he who would pass them.
In that space where time exists not,
faintly I sensed the guardians of cycles.
Move they only through angles.
Free are they not of the curved dimensions.

T8, V23.
Strange and terrible
are the HOUNDS of the Barrier.
Follow they consciousness to the limits of space.
Think not to escape by entering your body,
for follow they fast the Soul through angles.
Only the circle will give ye protection,
save from the claws
of the DWELLER IN ANGLES.

T8, V24.
Once, in a time past,
I approached the great Barrier,
and saw on the shores where time exists not,
the formless forms
of the HOUNDS of the barrier.
Aye, hiding in the mist beyond time I found them;
and THEY, scenting me afar off,
raised themselves and gave the great bell cry
that could be heard from cycle to cycle
and moved through space toward my soul.

Tablet Eight

T8, V25.
Fled I then fast before them,
back from time's unthinkable end.
But ever after me pursued they,
moving in strange angles not known to man.
Aye, on the gray shore of TIME-SPACE'S end
found I the HOUNDS of the Barrier,
ravening for the Soul
who attempts the beyond.

T8, V26.
Fled I through circles back to my body.
Fled, and fast after me they followed.
Aye, after me the devourers followed,
seeking through angles to devour my Soul.

T8, V27.
Aye, know ye man,
that the Soul who dares the Barrier
may be held in bondage
by the HOUNDS from beyond time,
held till this cycle is completed
and left behind
when the consciousness leaves.

T8, V28.
Entered I my body.
Created the circles that know not angles,
created the form
that from my form was formed.

Made my body into a circle
and lost the pursuers in the circles of time.
But, even yet, when free from my body,
cautious ever must I be
not to move through angles,
else my soul may never be free.

T8, V29.
Know ye, the HOUNDS of the Barrier
move only through angles
and never through curves of space.
Only by moving through curves
can ye escape them,
for in angles they will pursue thee.

T8, V30.
O man, heed ye my warning;
Seek not to break open
the gate to beyond.
Few there are
who have succeeded in passing the Barrier
to the greater LIGHT that shines beyond.
For know ye, ever the dwellers,
seek such Souls to hold in their thrall.

T8, V31.
Listen, O man, and heed ye my warning;
seek ye to move not in angles but curves,
And if while free from thy body,

thou hearest the sound like the bay of a hound
ringing clear and bell-like through thy being,
flee back to thy body through circles,
penetrate not the mist before.

T8, V32.
When thou hast entered the form thou hast dwelt in,
use thou the cross and the circle combined.
Open thy mouth and use thou thy Voice.
Utter the WORD and thou shalt be free.
Only the one who of LIGHT has the fullest
can hope to pass by the guards of the way.
And then must he move
through strange curves and angles
that are formed in direction not known to man.

T8, V33.
List ye, O man, and heed ye my warning:
attempt not to pass the guards in the way.
Rather should ye seek to gain of thine own Light
and make thyself ready to pass on the way.

T8, V34.
LIGHT is thine ultimate end, O my brother.
Seek and find ever the Light on the way.

Tablet Eight

NOTES

Chapter Nine

Emerald Tablet Nine:
The Key of Freedom of Space

Tablet 9, Verse 1.
List ye, O man, hear ye my voice,
teaching of Wisdom and Light in this cycle;
teaching ye how to banish the darkness,
teaching ye how to bring Light in thy life.

T9, V2.
Seek ye, O man, to find the great pathway
that leads to eternal LIFE as a SUN.
Draw ye away from the veil of the darkness.
Seek to become a Light in the world.
Make of thyself a vessel for Light,
a focus for the Sun of this space.

T9, V3.
Lift thou thine eyes to the Cosmos.
Lift thou thine eyes to the Light.
Speak in the words of the Dweller,
the chant that calls down the Light.

Sing thou the song of freedom.
Sing thou the song of the Soul.

T9, V4.
Create the high vibration
that will make thee One with the Whole.
Blend all thyself with the Cosmos.
Grow into ONE with the Light.
Be thou a channel of order,
a pathway of LAW to the world.

T9, V5.
Thy LIGHT, O man, is the great LIGHT,
shining through the shadow of flesh.
Free must thou rise from the darkness
before thou art One with the LIGHT.

T9, V6.
Shadows of darkness surround thee.
Life fills thee with its flow.
But know, O man, thou must arise
and forth from thy body go
far to the planes that surround thee
and yet are One with thee, too.

T9, V7.
Look all around thee, O man.
See thine own light reflected.
Aye, even in the darkness around thee,
thine own Light pours forth through the veil.

T9, V8.
Seek thou for wisdom always.
Let not thine body betray.
Keep in the path of the Light wave.
Shun thou the darkened way.
Know thee that wisdom is lasting,
existing since the ALL-SOUL began,
creating harmony from chaos
by the Law that exists in the WAY.

T9, V9.
List ye, O man, to the teaching of wisdom.
List to the voice that speaks of the past-time.
Aye, I shall tell thee knowledge forgotten,
tell ye of wisdom hidden in past-time,
lost in the mist of darkness around me.

T9, V10.
Know ye, man,
ye are the ultimate of all things.
Only the knowledge of this is forgotten,
lost when man was cast into bondage,
bound and fettered
by the chains of the darkness.

T9, V11.
Long, long ago, I cast off my body.
Wandered I free
through the vastness of ether,
circled the angles

that hold man in bondage.
Know ye, O man, ye are only a spirit.
The body is nothing.
The Soul is ALL.
Let not your body be a fetter.
Cast off the darkness and travel in Light.
Cast off your body, O man, and be free,
truly a Light that is ONE with the Light.

T9, V12.
When ye are free from the fetters of darkness
and travel in space as the SUN of the LIGHT,
then ye shall know that space in not boundless
but truly bounded by angles and curves.
Know ye, O man, that all that exists
is only an aspect of greater things yet to come.
Matter is fluid and flows like a stream,
constantly changing from one thing to another.

T9, V13.
All through the ages has knowledge existed;
never been changed, though buried in darkness;
never been lost, though forgotten by man.

T9, V14.
Know ye that throughout the space that ye dwell in
are others as great as your own,
interlaced through the heart of your matter
yet separate in space of their own.

Tablet Nine

T9, V15.
Once in a time long forgotten,
I, THOTH, opened the doorway,
penetrated into other spaces
and learned of the secrets concealed.
Deep in the essence of matter
are many mysteries concealed.

T9, V16.
Nine are the interlocked dimensions,
and Nine are the cycles of space.
Nine are the diffusions of consciousness,
and Nine are the worlds within worlds.
Aye, Nine are the Lords of the cycles
that come from above and below.

T9, V17.
Space is filled with concealed ones,
for space is divided by time.
Seek ye the key to the time-space,
and ye shall unlock the gate.
Know ye that throughout the time-space
consciousness surely exists.
Though from our knowledge it is hidden,
yet still forever exists.

T9, V18.
The key to worlds within thee
are found only within.

For man is the gateway of mystery
and the key that is One within One.

T9, V19.
Seek ye within the circle.
Use the WORD I shall give.
Open the gateway within thee,
and surely thou, too, shalt live.
Man, ye think that ye liveth,
but know it is life within death.
For as sure as ye are bound to your body,
for you no life exists.
Only the Soul is space-free,
has life that is really a life.
All else is only a bondage,
a fetter from which to be free.

T9, V20.
Think not that man is earth-born,
though come from the earth he may be.
Man is light-born spirit.
But, without knowing, he can never be free.
Darkness surrounds the light-born.
Darkness fetters the Soul.
Only the one who is seeking
may ever hope to be free.

T9, V21.
Shadows around thee are falling.
Darkness fills all the space.

Shine forth, O LIGHT of the man-soul.
Fill thou the darkness of space.
Ye are a SUN of the GREAT LIGHT.
Remember and ye shall be free.
Stay not thou in the shadows.
Spring forth from the darkness of night.
Light, let thy Soul be, O SUN-BORN,
fill with glory of Light,
freed from the bonds of the darkness,
a Soul that is One with the Light.

T9, V22.
Thou art the key to all wisdom.
Within thee is all time and space.
Live not in bondage to darkness.
Free thou thy Light-form from night.

T9, V23.
"Great Light that fills all the Cosmos,
flow thou fully to man.
Make of his body a light-torch
that shall never be quenched among men."

T9, V24.
Long in the past, sought I wisdom,
knowledge not known to man.
Far to the past, I traveled
into the space where time began.
Sought I ever new knowledge
to add to the wisdom I knew.

Yet only, I found, did the future
hold the key to the wisdom I sought.

T9, V25.
Down to the HALLS of AMENTI I journeyed,
the greater knowledge to seek.
Asked of the LORDS of the CYCLES,
the way to the wisdom I sought.
Asked the LORDS this question:
"Where is the source of ALL?"
Answered, in tones that were mighty,
the voice of the LORD of the NINE:
*"Free thou thy soul from thy body
and come forth with me to the LIGHT."*

T9, V26.
Forth I came from my body,
a glittering flame in the night.
Stood I before the LORDS,
bathed in the fire of LIFE.
Seized was I then by a force,
great beyond knowledge of man.
Cast was I to the Abyss
through spaces unknown to man.

T9, V27.
Saw I the molding of Order
from the chaos and angles of night.
Saw I the LIGHT spring from Order
and heard the voice of the Light.

Saw I the flame of the Abyss,
casting forth Order and Light.
Saw Order spring out of chaos.
Saw Light giving forth Life.

T9, V28.
Then heard I the voice:
"Hear thou and understand.
The flame is the source of all things,
containing all things in potentiality.
The Order that sent forth light is the WORD
and from the WORD comes LIFE
and the existence of all."
And again spoke the voice saying:
"THE LIFE in thee is the WORD.
Find thou the LIFE within thee,
and have powers to use of the WORD."

T9, V29.
Long I watched the Light-flame,
pouring forth from the Essence of Fire,
realizing that LIFE is but Order
and that man is one with the fire.

T9, V30.
Back I came to my body.
Stood again with the Nine,
listened to the voice of the CYCLES,
vibrate with powers they spoke:
"Know ye, O Thoth,

that LIFE is but the WORD of the FIRE.
The LIFE force ye seek before thee
is but the WORD in the World as a fire.
Seek ye the path to the WORD
and powers shall surely be thine."

T9, V31.
Then asked I of the Nine:
"O Lord, show me the path.
Give me the path to the wisdom.
Show me the way to the WORD."

T9, V32.
Answered me then, the LORD of the NINE:
"Through ORDER, ye shall find the way.
Saw ye not that the WORD came from Chaos?
Saw ye not that LIGHT came from FIRE?
Look in thy life for disorder.
Balance and order thy life.
Quell all the Chaos of emotions
and thou shalt have order in LIFE.
ORDER brought forth from Chaos
will bring thee the WORD of the SOURCE,
will give thee the power of CYCLES,
and make of thy Soul a force
that free will extend through the ages,
a perfected SUN from the Source."

Tablet Nine

T9, V33.
Listened I to the voice
and deep sank the words in my heart.
For ever have I sought for order
that I might draw on the WORD.
Know ye that he who attains it
must ever in ORDER be.
For use of the WORD though disorder
has never and can never be.

T9, V34.
Take ye these words, O man.
As part of thy life, let them be.
Seek thee to conquer disorder,
and One with the WORD thou shalt be.

T9, V35.
Put forth thy effort in gaining LIGHT
on the pathway of Life.
Seek to be One with the SUN-STATE.
Seek to be solely the LIGHT.
Hold thou thy thought on the Oneness
of Light with the body of man.
Know that all is Order from Chaos
born into Light.

Tablet Nine

NOTES

Chapter Ten

Emerald Tablet Ten:
The Key of Time

Tablet 10, Verse 1.
List ye, O Man. Take of my wisdom.
Learn of the deep hidden mysteries of space.
Learn of the THOUGHT that grew in the abyss,
bringing Order and Harmony in space.

T10, V2.
Know ye, O man, that all that exists
has being only because of the LAW.
Know ye the LAW and ye shall be free,
never be bound by the fetters of night.

T10, V3.
Far, through strange spaces, have I journeyed
into the depth of the abyss of time,
learning strange and yet stranger mysteries,
until in the end all was revealed.
Know ye that mystery is only mystery
when it is knowledge unknown to man.

When ye have plumbed the heart of all mystery,
knowledge and wisdom will surely be thine.

T10, V4.
Seek ye and learn that TIME is the secret
whereby ye may be free of this space.

T10, V5.
Long have I, THOTH, sought wisdom;
aye, and shall seek to eternity's end
for know I that ever before me receding
shall move the goal I seek to attain.
Even the LORDS of the CYCLES
know that not yet have THEY reached the goal,
For with all of their wisdom,
they know that TRUTH ever grows.

> Commentary: No one ever stops growing, stops seeking...there is always MORE...

T10, V6.
Once, in a past time, I spoke to the Dweller.
Asked of the mystery of time and space.
Asked him the question that surged
in my being, saying:
"O Master, what is time?"

T10, V7.
Then to me spoke HE, the Master:
*"Know ye, O Thoth, in the beginning
there was VOID and nothingness,
a timeless, spaceless, nothingness.
And into the nothingness came a thought,
purposeful, all-pervading,
and IT filled the VOID.
There existed no matter, only force,
a movement, a vortex, or vibration
of the purposeful thought
that filled the VOID."*

T10, V8.
And I questioned the Master, saying:
"Was this thought eternal?"
And answered me the DWELLER, Saying:
*"In the beginning, there was eternal thought,
and for thought to be eternal, time must exist.
So into the all-pervading thought
grew the LAW OF TIME.
Aye, time which exists through all space,
floating in a smooth, rhythmic movement
that is eternally in a state of fixation.
Time changes not,
but all things change in time.*

*For time is the force
that holds events separate,
each in its proper place.*

*Time is not in motion,
but ye move through time
as your consciousness
moves from one event to another.*

*Aye, by time ye exist, all in all,
an eternal ONE existence.
Know ye that even though in the time ye are separate,
yet still are ONE, in all times existent."*

T10, V9.
Ceased then the voice of the DWELLER,
and departed I to ponder on time.
For knew I that in these words lay wisdom
and a way to explore the mysteries of time.

T10, V10.
Oft did I ponder the words of the DWELLER.
Then sought I to solve the mystery of time.
Found I that time moves through strange angles.
Yet only by curves could I hope to attain the key
that would give me access to the time-space.
Found I that only by moving upward
and yet again by moving to right-ward
could I be free from the time of this movement.

T10, V11.
Forth I came from out of my body,
moved in the movements that changed me in time.

Strange were the sights I saw in my journeys,
many the mysteries that opened to view.
Aye, saw I man's beginning,
learned from the past that nothing is new.

T10, V12.
Seek ye, O man, to learn the pathway
that leads through the spaces
that are formed forth in time.

T10, V13.
Forget not, O man, with all of thy seeking
that Light is the goal ye shall seek to attain.
Search ye ever for Light on thy pathway
and ever for thee the goal shall endure.

T10, V14.
Let not thine heart turn ever to darkness.
Light let thine Soul be, a Sun on the way.
Know ye that in the eternal brightness,
ye shall ever find thy Soul hid in Light,
never fettered by bondage to darkness,
ever it shines forth a Sun of the Light.

T10, V15.
Aye, know, though hidden in darkness,
your Soul, a spark of the true flame, exists.
Be ye ONE with the greatest of all Lights.
Find at the SOURCE, the END of thy goal.

T10, V16.
Light is life, for without the great Light
nothing can ever exist.
Know ye, that in all formed matter,
the heart of Light always exists.
Aye, even though bound in the darkness,
inherent Light always exists.

T10, V17.
Once I stood in the HALLS OF AMENTI
and heard the voice of the LORDS OF AMENTI,
saying in tones that rang through the silence,
words of power, mighty and potent.
Chanted they the song of the cycles,
the words that open the path to beyond.
Aye, I saw the great path opened
and looked for an instant into the beyond.
Saw I the movements of the cycles,
vast as the thought of the SOURCE could convey.

T10, V18.
Knew I then that even Infinity
is moving on to some unthinkable end.
Saw I that the Cosmos is Order
and part of a movement that extends to all space,
a part of an Order of Orders,
constantly moving in a harmony of space.
Saw I the wheeling of cycles
like vast circles across the sky.
Knew I then that all that has being

is growing to meet yet other being
in a far-off grouping of space and of time.
Knew I then that in Words are power
to open the planes that are hidden from man.
Aye, that even in Words lie hidden the key
that will open above and below.

T10, V19.
Hark ye, now man, this word I leave with thee.
Use it and ye shall find power in its sound.
Say ye, the word:
"ZIN-URU"
and power ye shall find.
Yet must ye understand that man is of Light
and Light is of man.

T10, V20.
List ye, O man, and hear a mystery
stranger than all that lies 'neath the Sun.
Know ye, O man, that all space
is filled by worlds within worlds;
aye, one within the other yet separate by Law.

T10, V21.
Once in my search for deep buried wisdom,
I opened the door that bars THEM from man.
Called I from the other planes of being,
one who was fairer than the daughters of men.
Aye, I called her from out of the spaces
to shine as a Light in the world of men.

T10, V22.
Used I the drum of the Serpent.
Wore I the robe of the purple and gold.
Placed on my head, I, the crown of Silver.
Around me the circle of cinnabar shone.
Raised I my arms and cried the invocation
that opens the path to the planes beyond,
cried to the LORDS of the SIGNS in their houses:

T10, V23.
"Lords of the two horizons,
watchers of the treble gates,
stand ye One at the right and One at the left
as the STAR rises to his throne
and rules over his sign.
Aye, thou dark prince of ARULU,
open the gates of the dim, hidden land
and release her whom ye keep imprisoned."

T10, V24.
"Hear ye, hear ye, hear ye,
dark Lords and Shining Ones,
and by their secret names,
names which I know and can pronounce,
year ye and obey my will."

T10, V25.
Lit I then with flame my circle
and called HER

in the space-planes beyond.
Daughter of Light return from ARULU.
Seven times and seven times
have I passed through the fire.
Food have I not eaten.
Water have I not drunk.
I call thee from ARULU,
from the realms of EKERSHEGAL.
I summon thee, Lady of Light.

T10, V26.
Then before me rose the dark figures;
aye, the figures of the Lords of ARULU.
Parted they before me
and forth came the Lady of Light.

T10, V27.
Free was she now from the LORDS of the night,
free to live in the Light of the earth Sun,
free to live as a child of Light.

T10, V28.
Hear ye and listen, O my children.
Magic is knowledge and only is Law.
Be not afraid of the power within thee
for it follows Law as the stars in the sky.

T10, V29.
Know ye that to he without knowledge,

wisdom is magic and not of the Law.
But know ye that ever ye by your knowledge
can approach closer to a place in the Sun.

T10, V30.
List ye, my children, follow my teaching.
Be ye ever seekers of Light.
Shine in the world of men all around thee,
a Light on the path that shall shine among men.

T10, V31.
Follow ye and learn of my magic.
Know that all force is thine if thou wilt.
Fear not the path that leads thee to knowledge,
but rather shun ye the dark road.

T10, V32.
Light is thine, O man, for the taking.
Cast off the fetters and thou shalt be free.
Know ye that thy Soul is living in bondage
fettered by fear that holds ye in thrall.
Open thy eyes and see the great SUN-LIGHT.
Be not afraid for all is thine own.
Fear is the LORD of dark ARULU
to he who has never faced the dark fear.
Aye, know that fear has existence
created by those who are bound by their fears.

T10, V33.
Shake off thy bondage, O children,
and walk in the Light of the glorious day.
Never turn thy thoughts to the darkness
and surely ye shall be One with the Light.

T10, V34.
Man is only what he believeth,
a brother of darkness or a child of the Light.
Come thou into the Light my Children.
Walk in the pathway that leads to the Sun.

T10, V35.
Hark ye now, and list to the wisdom.
Use thou the word I have given unto thee.
Use it and surely thou shalt find power and wisdom
and Light to walk in the way.
Seek thee and find the key I have given
and ever shalt thou be a Child of the Light.

Tablet Ten

NOTES

Chapter Eleven

Emerald Tablet Eleven:
The Key to Above and Below

Tablet 11, Verse 1.
Hear ye and list ye,
O children of KHEM,
to the words that I give
that shall bring ye to Light.
Ye know, O men,
that I knew your fathers,
aye, your fathers in a time long ago.

Deathless have I been through all the ages,
living among ye
since your knowledge began.
Leading ye upward
to the Light of the Great Soul
have I ever striven,
drawing ye from out of the darkness of night.

T11, V2.
Know ye, O people amongst whom I walk,

that I, Thoth, have all of the knowledge
and all of the wisdom
known to man since the ancient days.
Keeper have I been
of the secrets of the great race,
holder of the key that leads into life.
Bringer up have I been to ye, O my children,
even from the darkness of the Ancient of Days.
List ye now to the words of my wisdom.
List ye now to the message I bring.
Hear ye now the words I give thee,
and ye shall be raised from the darkness to Light.

T11, V3.
Far in the past, when first I came to thee,
found I thee in caves of rocks.
Lifted I thee by my power and wisdom
until thou didst shine as men among men.
Aye, found I thee without any knowing.
Only a little were ye raised beyond beasts.
Fanned I ever the spark of thy consciousness
until at last ye flamed as men.

T11, V4.
Now shall I speak to thee knowledge
ancient beyond the thought of thy race.
Know ye that we of the Great Race
had and have knowledge
that is more than man's.

Wisdom we gained
from the star-born races,
wisdom and knowledge far beyond man's.
Down to us had descended masters of wisdom
as far beyond us as I am from thee.
List ye now while I give ye wisdom.
Use it and free thou shalt be.

T11, V5.
Know ye that in the pyramid I builded
are the KEYS that shall show ye the WAY into life.
Aye, draw ye a line
from the great image I builded,
to the apex of the pyramid, built as a gateway.
Draw ye another opposite
in the same angle and direction.
Dig ye and find that which I have hidden.
There shall ye find the underground entrance
to the secrets hidden before ye were men.

T11, V6.
Tell ye I now of the mystery of cycles
that move in movements
that are strange to the finite,
for infinite are they beyond knowledge of man.
Know ye that there are nine of the cycles;
aye, nine above and fourteen below,
moving in harmony to the place of joining
that shall exist in the future of time.

T11, V7.
Know ye that the LORDS of the CYCLES
are units of consciousness
sent from the others
to unify THIS with the ALL.
Highest are THEY
of the consciousness of all the CYCLES,
working in harmony with the LAW.
Know THEY that in time all will be perfected,
having none above and none below,
but all ONE in a perfected Infinity,
a harmony of all in the ONENESS of ALL.

T11, V8.
Deep 'neath the Earth's surface
in the HALLS of AMENTI
sit the Seven, the LORDS of the CYCLES,
aye, and another, the Lord from below.
Yet know thee that in Infinity
there is neither above nor below.
But ever there is and ever shall be
ONENESS of ALL when all is complete.
Oft have I journeyed to the HALLS OF AMENTI.
Oft have I stood before the LORDS of the ALL.
Oft at the fount of their wisdom have drunken
and filled both my body and Soul with their Light.

T11, V9.
Spake they to me and told me of cycles
and the LAW that gives them the means to exist.

Aye, spake to me the LORD of the NINE saying:
"O, Thoth, great are ye among Earth's children,
but mysteries exist of which ye know not.
Ye know that ye came from a space-time below this
and know ye shall travel to a space-time beyond.
But little ye know of the mysteries within them,
little ye know of the wisdom beyond.
Know ye that ye as a whole in this consciousness are
only a cell in the process of growth.

T11, V10.
The consciousness below thee is ever-expanding
in different ways from those known to thee.
Aye, it, though in space-time below thee,
is ever growing in ways that are different
from those that were part of the ways of thine own.
For know that it grows as a result of thy growth
but not in the same way that thou didst grow.
The growth that thou had and have in the present
have brought into being a cause and effect.

T11, V11.
No consciousness follows the path of those before it,
else all would be repetition and vain.
Each consciousness in the cycle it exists in
follows its own path to the ultimate goal.
Each plays its part in the Plan of the Cosmos.
Each plays its part in the ultimate end.
The farther the cycle, the greater its knowledge
and ability to blend the Law of the whole.

Tablet Eleven

T11, V12.
*Know ye, that ye in the cycles below us
are working the minor parts of the Law,
while we of the cycle that extends to Infinity
take of the striving and build greater Law.*

T11, V13.
*Each has his own part to play in the cycles.
Each has his work to complete in his way.
The cycle below thee is yet not below thee
but only formed for a need that exists.*

T11, V14.
*For know ye that the fountain of wisdom
that sends forth the cycles
is eternally seeking new powers to gain.*

T11, V15.
*Ye know that knowledge is gained only by practice,
and wisdom comes forth only from knowledge,
and thus are the cycles created by Law.
Means are they for the gaining of knowledge
for the Plane of Law that is the Source of the ALL.*

T11, V16.
*The cycle below is not truly below
but only different in space and in time.
The consciousness there is working and testing
lesser things than those ye are.*

T11, V17.
And know, just as ye are working on greater,
so above ye are those who are also working
as ye are on yet other laws.
The difference that exists between the cycles
is only in ability to work with the Law.

T11, V18.
We, who have being in cycles beyond thee,
are those who first came forth from the SOURCE
and have in the passage through time-space
gained ability to use Laws of the Greater
that are far beyond the conception of man.
Nothing there is that is really below thee
but only a different operation of Law.

T11, V19,
Look thee above or look thee below,
the same shall ye find.
For all is but part of the Oneness
that is at the Source of the Law.
The consciousness below thee is part thine own
as we are a part of thine.

T11, V20.
Ye, as a child had not the knowledge
that came to ye when ye became a man.
Compare ye the cycles to man in his journey
from birth unto death,
and see in the cycle below thee

*the child with the knowledge he has;
and see ye yourself as the child grown older,
advancing in knowledge as time passes on.*

T11, V21.
*See ye, We, also, the child grown to manhood
with the knowledge and wisdom
that came with the years.
So also, O Thoth, are the cycles of consciousness,
children in different stages of growth,
yet all from the one Source, the Wisdom,
and all to the Wisdom returning again."*

T11, V22.
Ceased then HE from speaking
and sat in the silence that comes to the LORDS.
Then again spake HE unto me, saying:
"O Thoth, long have We sat in Amenti,
guarding the flame of life in the Halls.
Yet know, we are still part of our Cycles
with our Vision reaching unto them and beyond.
Aye, know we that of all, nothing else matters
excepting the growth we can gain with our Soul.
Know we the flesh is fleeting.
The things men count great are nothing to us.
The things we seek are not of the body
but are only the perfected state of the Soul.

T11, V23.
When ye as men can learn that nothing

*but progress of Soul can count in the end,
then truly ye are free from all bondage,
free to work in a harmony of Law.*

T11, V24.
*Know, O man, ye should aim at perfection,
for only thus can ye attain to the goal.
Though ye should know that nothing is perfect,
yet it should be thy aim and thy goal."*

T11, V25.
Ceased again the voice of the Nine,
and into my consciousness the words had sunk.
Now, seek I ever more wisdom
that I may be perfect in Law with the ALL.

T11, V26.
Soon go I down to the Halls of Amenti
to live 'neath the cold flower of life.
Ye whom I have taught shall nevermore see me.
Yet live I forever in the wisdom I taught.

T11, V27.
All that man is, is because of his wisdom.
All that he shall be, is the result of his cause.

T11, V28.
List ye, now to my voice
and become greater than common man.
Lift thine eyes upward,

let Light fill thy being,
be thou ever Children of Light.
Only by effort shall ye grow upward
to the plane where Light is the ALL of the ALL.
Be ye the master of all that surrounds thee.
Never be mastered by the effects of thy life.
Create then ever more perfect causes
and in time shalt thou be a Sun of the Light.

T11, V29.
Free, let thine soul soar ever upward,
free from the bondage and fetters of night.
Lift thine eyes to the Sun in the sky-space.
For thee, let it be a symbol of life.
Know that thou art the Great Light,
perfect in thine own sphere, when thou art free.

T11, V30.
Look not ever into the blackness.
Lift up thine eyes to the space above.
Free let thine Light flame upward
and shalt thou be a Child of the LIGHT.

NOTES

Chapter Twelve

Emerald Tablet Twelve:
The Law of Cause and Effect and
The Key of Prophecy

Tablet 12, Verse 1.
List ye, O man, to the words of my wisdom,
list to the voice of Thoth, the Atlantean.
Conquered have I the Law of the time-space.
Knowledge have I gained of the future of time.
Know I that man
in his movement through space-time
shall ever be ONE with the ALL.

T12, V2.
Know ye, O man, that all of the future
is an open book to him who can read.
All effect shall bring forth its causes
as all effects grew from the first cause.
Know ye the future is not fixed or stable
but varies as cause brings forth an effect.
Look in the cause thou shalt bring into being,
and surely thou shalt see that all is effect.

T12, V3.
In the great beginning, there grew the First Cause
that brought into being all that exists.
Thou, thyself, are the effect of causation
and in turn are the cause of yet other effects.

T12, V4.
So, O man, be sure the effects that ye bring forth
are ever causes of more perfect effects.
Know ye the future is never in fixation
but follows man's free will as it moves
through the movements of time-space
toward the goal where a new time begins.
Man can only read the future
through the causes that bring the effects.
Seek ye within the causation
and surely ye shall find the effects.

T12, V5.
List ye, O man, while I speak of the future,
speak of the effect that follows the cause.
Know ye that man in his journey light-ward
is ever seeking escape from the night.

Aye, from the blackness of night
that surrounds him,
like the shadows that surround the stars in the sky
and like the stars in the sky-space,
he, too, shall shine from the shadows of night.

T12, V6.
Ever his destiny shall lead him onward
until he is ONE with the Light.
Aye, though his way lies midst the shadows,
ever before him glows the Great Light.
Dark though the way be, yet shall he conquer
the shadows that flow around him like night.

T12, V7.
Far in the future, I see men as Light-born,
free from the darkness that fetters the Soul,
living in Light without the bonds of the darkness
to cover the Light that is Light of their Soul.

Know ye, O man, before ye attain this
that many the dark shadows shall fall on your Light
striving to quench with the shadows of darkness
the Light of the Soul that strives to be free.

T12, V8.
Great is the struggle between Light and darkness,
age old and yet ever new.
Yet, know in a time, far in the future,
Light shall be All and darkness shall fall.

T12, V9.
List ye, O man, to my words of wisdom.
Prepare and ye shall not bind your Light.
Man has risen and man has fallen
as ever new waves of consciousness flow

from the great abyss below us
toward the Sun of their goal.

T12, V10.
Ye, my children, have risen from a state
that was little above the beast,
until now of all men ye are greatest.
Yet before thee were others greater than thee.
Yet tell I thee as before thee others have fallen,
so also shall ye come to an end.
And upon the land where ye dwell now,
barbarians shall dwell and in turn rise to Light.
Forgotten shall be the ancient-wisdom,
yet ever shall live though hidden from men.

T12, V11.
Aye, in the land thou callest Khem,
races shall rise and races shall fall.
Forgotten shalt thou be of the children of men.
Yet thou shalt have moved
to a star-space beyond this
leaving behind this place where thou hast dwelt.

T12, V12.
The Soul of man moves ever onward,
bound not by any one star.
But ever moving to the great goal before him
where he is dissolved in the Light of the All.
Know ye that ye shall ever go onward,

moved by the Law of cause and effect
until in the end both become One.

T12, V13.
Aye, man, after ye have gone,
others shall move in the places ye lived.
Knowledge and wisdom shall all be forgotten,
and only a memory of Gods shall survive.
As I to thee am a God by my knowledge,
so ye, too, shall be Gods of the future
because of your knowledge far above theirs.
Yet know ye that all through the ages,
man shall have access to Law when he will.

T12, V14.
Ages to come shall see revival of wisdom
to those who shall inherit thy place on this star.
They shall, in turn, come into wisdom
and learn to banish the darkness by Light.

Yet greatly must they strive through the ages
to bring unto themselves the freedom of Light.
Many who are bound in darkness
Shall strive to hold others from Light.
Then shall there come unto man the great warfare
that shall make the Earth tremble
and shake in its course.
Aye, then shall the Dark Brothers open the warfare
between Light and the night.

T12, V15.
When man again shall conquer the ocean
and fly in the air on wings like the birds;
when he has learned to harness the lightning,
then shall the time of warfare begin.

T12, V16.
Great shall the battle be twixt the forces,
great the warfare of darkness and Light.
Nation shall rise against nation
using the dark forces to shatter the Earth.
Weapons of force shall wipe out the Earth-men
until half of the races of men shall be gone.

T12, V17.
Then shall come forth the Sons of the Morning
and give their edict to the children of men, saying:

"O men, cease from thy striving against thy brother.
Only thus can ye come to the Light.
Cease from thy unbelief, O my brother,
and follow the path and know ye are right."

T12, V18.
Then shall men cease from their striving,
brother against brother and father against son.
Then shall the ancient home of my people
rise from its place 'neath the dark ocean waves.
Then shall the Age of Light be unfolded
with all men seeking the Light of the goal.

Then shall the Brothers of Light rule the people.
Banished shall be the darkness of night.

T12, V19.
Aye, the children of men shall progress
onward and upward to the great goal.
Children of Light shall they become.
Flame of the flame shall their Souls ever be.

T12, V20.
Knowledge and wisdom
shall be man's in the great age
for he shall approach the eternal flame,
the SOURCE of all wisdom, the place of beginning,
that is yet ONE with the end of all things.
Aye, in a time that is yet unborn,
all shall be ONE and ONE shall be All.
Man, a perfect flame of this Cosmos,
shall move forward to a place in the stars.
Aye, shall move even from out of this space-time
into another beyond the stars.

T12, V21.
Long have ye listened to me, O my children,
long have ye listened to the wisdom of Thoth.
Now I depart from ye into darkness.

Now go I to the HALLS of AMENTI,
there to dwell in the future

(when) Light shall come again to man.
Yet, know ye, my Spirit shall ever be with thee,
guiding thy feet in the pathway of Light.

T12, V22.
Guard ye the secrets I leave with thee,
and surely my spirit will guard thee through life.
Keep thine eyes ever on the pathway to wisdom.
Keep the Light as thy goal evermore.
Fetter not thy Soul in bondage of darkness;
free let it wing in its flight to the stars.

T12, V23.
Now I depart thee to dwell in Amenti.
Be thou my children in this life and the next.
The time will come when ye, too, shall be deathless,
living from age to age a Light among men.

T12, V24.
Guard ye the entrance to the HALLS of AMENTI.
Guard ye the secrets I have hidden among ye.
Let not the wisdom be cast to barbarians.
Secret shall thou keep it for those who seek Light.
Now depart I.

T12, V25.
Receive thou my blessing.
Take thou my way and follow the Light.
Blend thou thy Soul in the Great Essence.

*ONE with the Great Light let thy consciousness be.
Call thou on me when thou dost need me.
Use my name three times in a row:
CHEQUETET, ARELICH, VOMALITES.*

NOTES

Chapter Thirteen

Emerald Tablet Thirteen:
The Keys of Life and Death

Tablet 13, Verse 1.
List ye, O man, hear ye the wisdom.
Hear ye the Word that shall fill thee with Life.
Hear ye the Word that shall banish the darkness.
Hear ye the voice that shall banish the night.

T13, V2.
Mystery and wisdom
have I brought to my children;
knowledge and power descended from old.
Know ye not that all shall be opened
when ye shall find the oneness of all?
One shall ye be with the Masters of Mystery,
Conquerors of Death and Masters of Life.
Aye, ye shall learn of the flower of Amenti
the blossom of life that shines in the Halls.

T13, V3.
In Spirit shall ye reach that Halls of Amenti

and bring back the wisdom that liveth in Light.
Know ye the gateway to power is secret.
Know ye the gateway to life is through death.
Aye, through death but not as ye know death,
but a death that is life and is fire and is Light.

T13, V4.
Desireth thou to know the deep, hidden secret?
Look in thy heart where the knowledge is bound.
Know that in thee the secret is hidden,
the source of all life and the source of all death.

T13, V5.
List ye, O man, while I tell the secret,
reveal unto thee the secret of old.

T13, V6.
Deep in Earth's heart lies the flower,
the source of the Spirit that binds all in its form.
For know ye that the Earth is living in body
as thou art alive in thine own formed form.

T13, V7.
The Flower of Life
is as thine own place of Spirit
and streams through the Earth
as thine flows through thy form;
giving of life to the Earth and its children,
renewing the Spirit from form unto form.

This is the Spirit that is form of thy body,
shaping and molding into its form.

T13, V8.
Know ye, O man, that thy form is dual,
balanced in polarity while formed in its form.
Know that when fast on thee DEATH approaches,
it is only because thy balance is shaken.
It is only because one pole has been lost.

T13, V9.
Know that thy body when in perfect balance
May never be touched by the finger of DEATH.
Aye, even accident may only approach
when the balance is gone.
When ye are in a balanced equilibrium,
ye shall live on in time and not taste of Death.
Know that thou art the balanced completion,
existing because of thy balance of poles.
As, in thee, one pole is drawn downward,
fast from thee goes the balance of life.
Then unto thee, cold death approaches,
and change must come to thine unbalanced life.

T13, V10.
Know that the secret of life in AMENTI
is the secret of restoring the balance of poles.
All that exists has form and is living
because of the Spirit of life in its poles.

T13, V11.
See ye not that in Earth's heart is the balance
of all things that exist and have being on its face?
The source of thy Spirit is drawn from Earth's heart,
for in thy form thou art one with the Earth.

T13, V12.
When thou hast learned to hold thine own balance,
then shalt thou draw on the balance of Earth.
Exist then shalt thou while Earth is existing,
changing in form, only when Earth, too, shalt change:
Tasting not of death, but one with this planet,
holding thy form till all pass away.

T13, V13.
List ye, O man, whilst I give the secret
so that ye, too, shalt taste not of change.
One hour each day shalt thou lie with thine head
pointed to the place of the positive pole (north).
One hour each day shalt thy head be pointed
to the place of the negative pole (south).
Whilst thy head is placed to the northward,
hold thou thy consciousness
from the chest to the head.

T13, V14.
And when thy head is placed southward,
hold thou thy thought from chest to the feet.

*Hold thou in balance once in each seven,
and thy balance will retain the whole of its strength.
Aye, if thou be old, thy body will freshen
and thy strength will become as a youth's.
This is the secret known to the Masters
by which they hold off the fingers of Death.
Neglect not to follow the path I have shown,
for when thou hast passed beyond years to a hundred
to neglect it will mean the coming of Death.*

T13, V15.
Hear ye, my words, and follow the pathway.
Keep thou thy balance and live on in life.

T13, V16.
Hear ye, O man, and list to my voice.
List to the wisdom that gives thee of Death.
When at the end of thy work appointed,
thou may desire to pass from this life,
pass to the plane where the Suns of the Morning
live and have being as Children of Light.
Pass without pain and pass without sorrow
into the plane where is eternal Light.

T13, V17.
*First lie at rest with thine head to the eastward.
Fold thou thy hands at the Source of thy life
(solar plexus).*

T13, V18.
Place thou thy consciousness in the life seat.
Whirl it and divide to north and to south.

T13, V19.
Send thou the one out toward the northward.
Send thou the other out to the south.

T13, V20.
Relax thou thy hold upon thy being.
Forth from thy form will thy silver spark fly,
upward and onward to the Sun of the morning,
blending with Light, at one with its source.

T13, V21.
There it shall flame till desire shall be created.
Then shall return to a place in a form.

T13, V22.
Know ye, O men,
that thus pass the great Souls,
changing at will from life unto life.
Thus ever passes the Avatar,
willing his Death as he wills his own life.

T13, V23.
{The key to the placing of consciousness
at the time of death so that memory may be carried
from one incarnation to another.}

Tablet Thirteen

T13, V24.
List ye, O man, drink of my wisdom.
Learn ye the secret that is Master of TIME.
Learn ye how those ye call Masters
are able to remember the lives of the past.

T13, V25.
Great is the secret yet easy to master,
giving to thee the mastery of time.
When upon thee death fast approaches,
fear not but know ye are master of Death.

T13, V26.
Relax thy body, resist not with tension.
Place in thy heart the flame of thy Soul.
Swiftly then sweep it to the seat of the triangle.

T13, V27.
Hold for a moment, then move to the goal.
This, thy goal, is the place between thine eyebrows,
the place where the memory of life must hold sway.

T13, V28.
Hold thou thy flame here in thy brain-seat
until the fingers of Death grasp thy Soul.
Then as thou pass through the state of transition,
surely the memories of life shall pass, too.

Tablet Thirteen

T13, V29.
Then shall the past be as one with the present.
Then shall the memory of all be retained.
Free shalt thou be from all retrogression.
The things of the past shall live in today.

T13, V30.
Man, ye have heard the voice of my wisdom.
Follow, and ye shall live through the ages as I.

NOTES

Chapter Fourteen

Emerald Tablet Fourteen:
Becoming Thrice Greatest

Tablet 14, Verse 1.
List ye, O Man, to the deep hidden wisdom,
lost to the world since the time of the Dwellers,
lost and forgotten by men of this age.

T14, V2.
Know ye this Earth is but a portal,
guarded by powers unknown to man.
Yet, the Dark Lords hide the entrance
that leads to the Heaven-born land.
Know ye, the way to the sphere of Arulu
is guarded by barriers
opened only to Light-born man.

T14, V3.
Upon Earth, I am the holder of the keys
to the gates of the Sacred Land.
Commanded I, by the powers beyond me,
to leave the keys to the world of man.

Tablet Fourteen

Before I depart, I give ye the Secrets
of how ye may rise from the bondage of
darkness, cast off the fetters of flesh that
have bound ye, rise from the darkness into
the Light.

T14, V4.
Know ye, the soul must be cleansed of its
darkness, ere ye may enter the portals of Light.
Thus, I established among ye the Mysteries
so that the Secrets may always be found.
Aye, though men may fall into darkness,
always the Light will shine as a guide.
Hidden in darkness, veiled in symbols,
always the way to the portal will be found.
Man in the future will deny the mysteries
but always the way the seeker will find.

T14, V5.
Now I command ye to maintain my secrets,
giving only to those ye have tested,
so that the pure may not be corrupted,
so that the power of Truth may prevail.

T14, V6.
List ye now to the unveiling of Mystery.
List to the symbols of Mystery I give.
Make of it a religion
for only thus will its essence remain.

T14, V7.
Regions, there are two
between this life and the Great One,
traveled by the Souls who depart from this Earth;
DUAT, the home of the powers of illusion;
SEKHET HETSPET, the House of the Gods.
OSIRIS, the symbol of the guard of the portal,
who turns back the souls of unworthy men.

T14, V8.
Beyond lies the sphere
of the heaven-born powers,
ARULU, the land
where the Great Ones have passed.
There, when my work among men
has been finished, will I join
the Great Ones of my Ancient home.

T14, V9.
SEVEN are the mansions
of the house of the Mighty;
THREE guards the portal
of each house from the darkness;
FIFTEEN the ways that lead to Duat.

T14, V10.
TWELVE are the houses
of the Lords of Illusion,
facing four ways, each of them different.

Tablet Fourteen

T14, V11.
FORTY and TWO are the great powers,
judging the Dead who seek for the portal.

T14, V12.
FOUR are the Sons of Horus,
TWO are the Guards of East and West-
ISIS, the mother
who pleads for her children,
Queen of the moon, reflecting the Sun.

T14, V13.
BA is the essence, living forever.
KA is the Shadow that man knows as life.
Ba cometh not, until Ka is incarnate.

T14, V14.
These are mysteries
to preserve through the ages.
Keys are they of Life and of Death.
Hear ye now the mystery of mysteries:
learn of the circle
beginningless and endless,
the form of He who is One and in all.

T14, V15.
Listen and hear it,
go forth and apply it,
thus will ye travel the way that I go.
Mystery in Mystery,

yet clear to the Light-born,
the Secret of all, I now will reveal.
I will declare a secret to the initiated,
but let the door be wholly
shut against the profane.

T14, V16.
Three is the mystery,
come from the great one.
Hear, and Light on thee will dawn.

T14, V17.
In the primeval, dwell three unities.
Other than these, none can exist.
These are the equilibrium,
source of creation:
one God, one Truth, one point of freedom.

T14, V18.
Three come forth from the three of the balance:
all life, all good, all power.

T14, V19.
Three are the qualities of God in his Light-home :
Infinite power, Infinite Wisdom, Infinite Love.

T14, V20.
Three are the powers given to the Masters:
To transmute evil, assist good, use discrimination.

Tablet Fourteen

T14, V21.
Three are the things inevitable for God to perform:
Manifest power, wisdom and love.

T14, V22.
Three are the powers creating all things:
<u>Divine Love</u> possessed of perfect knowledge,
<u>Divine Wisdom</u> knowing all possible means,
<u>Divine Power</u> possessed by the joint will
of Divine Love and Wisdom.

T14, V23.
Three are the circles (or states) of existence:
The <u>circle of Light</u> where dwells nothing but God,
and only God can traverse it;
the <u>circle of Chaos</u>
where all things by nature arise from death;
The <u>circle of Awareness</u>
where all things spring from life.

T14, V24.
All things animate are of three states of existence:
<u>chaos or death</u>,
<u>liberty in humanity</u> and <u>felicity of Heaven</u>.

T14, V25.
Three necessities control all things:
<u>beginning in the Great Deep</u>,
the <u>circle of chaos</u>, <u>plenitude in Heaven</u>.

T14, V26.
Three are the paths of the Soul:
Man, Liberty, Light.

T14, V27.
Three are the hindrances:
lack of endeavor to obtain knowledge;
non-attachment to God;
attachment to evil.
In man, the three are manifest.

T14, V28.
Three are the Kings of power within.
Three are the chambers of the mysteries,
found yet not found in the body of man.

T14, V29.
Hear ye now of he who is liberated,
freed from the bondage of life into Light.
Knowing the source
of all worlds shall be open.
Aye, even the Gates of Arulu
shall not be barred.

T14, V30.
Yet heed, O man, who wouldst enter heaven.
If ye be not worthy,
better it be to fall into the fire.
Know ye the Celestials
pass through the pure flame.

Tablet Fourteen

At every revolution of the heavens,
they bathe in the fountains of Light.

T14, V31.
List ye, O man, to this mystery:
Long in the past before ye were man-born,
I dwelled in Ancient Atlantis.
There in the Temple, I drank of the Wisdom,
poured as a fountain of Light
from the Dweller.
Give the key to ascend
to the Presence of Light in the Great world.

Stood I before the Holy (One)
enthroned in the flower of fire.
Veiled was he by the lightnings of darkness,
else my Soul by the Glory
have been shattered.

T14, V32.
Forth from the feet of his Throne
like the diamond,
rolled forth four rivers of flame
from his footstool,
rolled through the channels of clouds
to the Man-world.

T14, V33.
Filled was the hall with Spirits of Heaven.
Wonder of wonders was the Starry palace.

Above the sky,
like a rainbow of Fire and Sunlight,
were formed the spirits.

T14, V34.
Sang they the glories of the Holy One.
Then from the midst of the Fire came a voice:
"Behold the Glory of the First Cause."
I beheld that Light, high above all darkness,
reflected in my own being.
I attained, as it were, to the God of all Gods,
the Spirit-Sun,
the Sovereign of the Sun spheres.

T14, V35.
Again came the Voice:
"There is one, even the First,
who hath no beginning, who hath no end;
who hath made all things, who governs all,
who is good, who is just,
who illumines, who sustains."

T14, V36.
Then from the throne,
there poured a great radiance,
surrounding and lifting my soul by its power.
Swiftly I moved through the spaces of Heaven,
shown was I the mystery of mysteries,
shown the Secret heart of the cosmos.

Tablet Fourteen

T14, V37.
Carried was I to the land of Arulu,
stood before the Lords in their Houses.
Opened they the Doorway
so I might glimpse the primeval chaos.
Shuddered my soul to the vision of horror,
shrank back my soul
from the ocean of darkness.

T14, V38.
Then saw I the need for the barriers,
saw the need for the Lords of Arulu.
Only they with their Infinite balance
Could stand in the way of the inpouring chaos.
Only they could guard God's creation.

T14, V39.
Then did I pass 'round the circle of eight.
Saw all the souls who had conquered the darkness.
Saw the splendor of Light where they dwelled.

T14, V40.
Longed I to take my place in their circle,
but longed I also for the way I had chosen,
when I stood in the Halls of Amenti
and made my choice to the work I would do.

> Commentary: Thoth chose here to be a teacher of man.

T14, V41.
Passed I from the Halls of Arulu
down to the earth space where my body lay.
Arose I from the Earth where I rested.
Stood I before the Dweller.
Gave my pledge to renounce my Great Right
until my work on Earth was completed,
until the Age of darkness be past.

T14, V42.
List ye, O man, to the words I shall give ye.
In them shall ye find the Essence of Life.
Before I return to the Halls of Amenti,
taught shall ye be the Secrets of Secrets,
how ye, too, may arise to the Light.
Preserve them and guard them,
hide them in symbols,
so the profane will laugh and renounce.
In every land, form ye the mysteries.
Make the way hard for the seeker to tread.
Thus will the weak
and the wavering be rejected.

T14, V43.
Thus will the secrets be hidden and guarded,
held till the time
when the wheel shall be turned.

Tablet Fourteen

T14, V44.
Through the dark ages,
waiting and watching,
my Spirit shall remain
in the deep hidden land.
When one has passed
all the trials of the outer,
summon ye me by the Key that ye hold.
Then will I, the Initiator, answer,
come from the Halls of the Gods in Amenti.
Then will I receive the initiate,
give him the words of power.

T14, V45.
Hark ye, remember, these words of warning:
bring not to me one lacking in wisdom,
impure in heart or weak in his purpose.
Else I will withdraw from ye your power
to summon me from the place of my sleeping.

T14, V46.
Go forth and conquer
the element of darkness.
Exalt in thy nature thine essence of Light.

T14, V47.
Now go ye forth and summon thy brothers
so that I may impart the wisdom
to light thy path when my presence is gone.

T14, V48.
Come to the chamber beneath my temple.
Eat not food until three days are past.
There will I give thee the essence of wisdom
so that with power
ye may shine amongst men.
There will I give unto thee the secrets
so that ye, too, may rise to the Heavens-
God-men in Truth as in essence ye be.
Depart now and leave me
while I summon those ye know of
but as yet know not.

Tablet Fourteen

NOTES

Chapter Fifteen

Emerald Tablet Fifteen:
Secret of Secrets

Tablet 15, Verse 1.
Now ye assemble, my children,
waiting to hear the Secret of Secrets
which shall give ye power to unfold the God-man,
give ye the way to Eternal life.
Plainly shall I speak of the Unveiled Mysteries.
No dark sayings shall I give unto thee.
Open thine ears now, my children.
Hear and obey the words that I give.

T15, V2.
First I shall speak of the fetter of darkness
which bind ye in chains to the sphere of the Earth.

T15, V3.
Darkness and Light are both of one nature,
different only in seeming,
for each arose from the source of all.
Darkness is disorder.

Light is Order.
Darkness transmuted is light of the Light.
This, my children, your purpose in being;
transmutation of darkness to Light.

T15, V4.
Hear ye now of the mystery of nature,
the relations of life to the Earth where it dwells.
Know ye, ye are threefold in nature,
<u>physical</u>, <u>astral</u> and <u>mental</u> in one.
Three are the qualities of each of the natures;
nine in all, as above, so below.

T15, V5.
In the physical are these channels,
the <u>blood</u> which moves in <u>vortical motion</u>,
reacting on the heart to continue its beating.

T15, V6.
<u>Magnetism</u> which moves through the <u>nerve paths</u>,
carrier of energies to all cells and tissues.

T15, V7.
<u>Akasa</u> which flows through <u>channels</u>,
subtle yet physical, completing the channels.

T15, V8.
Each of the three attuned with each other,
each affecting the life of the body.

Form they the Skeletal framework
through which the subtle ether flows.

T15, V9.
In their mastery lies the Secret of Life in the body.
Relinquished only by will of the adept,
when his purpose in living is done.

T15, V10.
Three are the natures of the Astral,
<u>mediator</u> is between <u>above and below</u>;
not of the physical, not of the Spiritual,
but able to move above and below.

T15, V11.
Three are the natures of Mind,
carrier it is of the Will of the Great One.
Arbitrator of Cause and Effect in thy life.
Thus is formed the threefold being,
directed from above by the power of four.

T15, V12.
Above and beyond man's threefold nature
lies the realm of the Spiritual Self.
Four is it in qualities,
shining in each of the planes of existence,
but thirteen in one, the mystical number.

T15, V13.
Based on the qualities of man
are the Brothers:
each shall direct the unfoldment of being,
each shall channels be of the Great One.

T15, V14.
On Earth, man is in bondage,
bound by space and time to the earth plane.
Encircling each planet, a wave of vibration,
binds him to his plane of unfoldment.
Yet within man is the Key to releasement,
within man may freedom be found.

T15, V15.
When ye have released the self from the body,
rise to the outermost bounds
of your earth-plane.
Speak ye the word DOR-E-UL-LA.
Then for a time your Light will be lifted,
free may ye pass the barriers of space.

T15, V16.
For a time of half of the sun (six hours),
free may ye pass the barriers of earth-plane,
see and know those who are beyond thee.
Yea, to the highest worlds may ye pass.
See your own possible heights of unfoldment,
know all earthly futures of Soul.

Tablet Fifteen

T15, V17.
Bound are ye in your body,
but by the power ye may be free.
This is the Secret whereby bondage
shall be replaced by freedom for thee.

T15, V18.
Calm let thy mind be.
At rest be thy body:
Conscious only of freedom from flesh.
Center thy being on the goal of thy longing.
Think over and over that thou wouldst be free.
Think of this word-LA-UM-I-L-GAN-
over and over in thy mind let it sound.
Drift with the sound to the place of thy longing.
Free from the bondage of flesh by thy will.

T15, V19.
Hear ye while I give the greatest of secrets:
how ye may enter the Halls of Amenti,
enter the place of the immortals as I did,
stand before the Lords in their places.

T15, V20.
Lie ye down in rest of thy body.
Calm thy mind so no thought disturbs thee.
Pure must ye be in mind and in purpose,
else only failure will come unto thee.

T15, V21.
Vision Amenti as I have told in my Tablets.
Long with fullness of heart to be there.
Stand before the Lords in thy mind's eye.
Pronounce the words of power I give (mentally);
MEKUT-EL-SHAB-EL HALE-ZUR-BEN-EL-ZABRUT
ZIN-EFRIM-QUAR-EL.
Relax thy mind and thy body.
Then be sure your soul will be called.

T15, V22.
Now give I the Key to Shamballa,
the place where my Brothers live in the darkness:
Darkness but filled with Light of the Sun-
Darkness of Earth, but Light of the Spirit,
guides for ye when my day is done.

T15, V23.
Leave thou thy body as I have taught thee.
Pass to the barriers of the deep, hidden place.
Stand before the gates and their guardians.
Command thy entrance by these words:

T15, V24.
"I am the Light.
In me is no darkness.
Free am I of the bondage of night.
Open thou the way of the Twelve and the One,
so I may pass to the realm of wisdom."

When they refuse thee, as surely they will,
command them to open by these words of power:

T15, V25.
"I am the Light.
For me are no barriers.
Open, I command, by the Secret of Secrets-
EDOM-EL-AHIM-SABBERT-ZUR ADOM."
Then if thy words have been "Truth"
of the highest,
open for thee the barriers will fall.

T15, V26.
Now, I leave thee, my children.
Down, yet up, to the Halls shall I go.
Win ye the way to me, my children.
Truly my brothers shall ye become.

T15, V27.
Thus finish I my writings.
Keys let them be to those who come after.
But only to those who seek my wisdom,
for only for these am I the Key and the Way.

NOTES

Chapter Sixteen

Index of Common Search Terms

Angle(s) - T8, V22, 23(2), 25, 26, 28(2), 29(2), 31, 32.
     T9, V11,12, 27.
     T10, V10.

Awareness - T14, V23.

Barrier(s) - T7, V24.
     T8, V22(2), 23, 24(2), 25, 27, 29, 30.
     T14, V2, 38.
     T15, V15,16, 23, 25(2).

Brother(s) - T2, V15,21.
     T3, V22.
     T6, V6, 8(2), 9,10(2),12,14(3),15, 20,
        25(2), 26.
     T7, V30.
     T8, V5, 21,34.
     T10, V34.
     T12, V14, 17(2),18(3).
     T14, V47.
     T15, V13, 22, 26.

Index of Common Search Terms

Circle(s)(d) - T1, V15.
        T2, V10.
        T4, V4.
        T6, V23(2).
        T7, V18.
        T8, V23, 26, 28(3), 31, 32.
        T9, V11, 19.
        T10, V18, 22, 25.
        T14, V14, 23(4), 25, 39, 40.

Conscious(ness) - T1, V16.
        T3, V23.
        T4, V20,21,24.
        T7, V12,24.
        T8, V23,27.
        T9, V16,17.
        T10, V8.
        T11,V3,7(2),9,10,11(2),16,19,21,25.
        T12, V9,25.
        T13, V13,18,23.
        T15, V18.

Dark Lords - T10, V24.
        T14, V2.

Dweller(s) - T1, V9,11,12,17,25,29(2).
        T2, V16,31.
        T5, V7,13(2),14(2),17,21,22,23,26.
        T6, V8.

Index of Common Search Terms

        T7, V11.
        T8, V5,23,30.
        T9, V3.
        T10, V6,8,9,10.
        T14, V1,31,41.

Flame(s)(ed) - T1, V10,15.
        T2, V9,21(3),22(3),24,25(2),26.
        T3, V34,45.
        T4, V13(2),22(2),23,25,26.
        T6, V4(2).
        T7, V5,11,13(4),21,29.
        T8, V8(3),10,11(2).
        T9, V26,27,28,29.
        T10, V15,25.
        T11, V3,22,30.
        T12, V19(2),20(2).
        T13, V21,26,28.
        T14, V30,32.

Flower(s) -T1, V17(2).
        T2, V7,12,13,22,24.
        T3, V29,42.
        T4, V20.
        T6, V23.
        T11, V26.
        T13, V2,6,7.
        T14, V31.

Index of Common Search Terms

Food - T3, V16.
    T4, V20.
    T10, V25.
    T14, 48.

God(s) - T12, V13(3).
    T14, V7,17,19,21,23(2),27,34(2),38,44,48.
    T15, V1.

Horlet - T5, V4.

Hounds - T8, V22,23,24,25,27,29.

Key(s) - Doreal's Introduction(4)
    T1, V14,27.
    T3, V33,35,37,40,41.
    T4, V29.
    T5, V4,30(3).
    T8, V4,5.
    T9, V17,18(2),22,24.
    T10, V10,18,35
    T11, V2,5.
    T13, V23.
    T14, V3(2),14,31,44.
    T15, V14,22,27(2).

Lady - T10, V25,26.

Law(s) - Doreal's Introduction(8)
    T1, V17.
    T3, V4(2),26(3).
    T4, V4,5,19,24.
    T5, V17.
    T6, V14.
    T7, V7,14,15,18.
    T8, V7.
    T9, V4,8.
    T10, V2(2),8,20,28(2),29.
    T11, V7,9,11,12(2),15(2),17(2),18(2),19,23,25.
    T12, V1,12,13.

Mind - Doreal's Introduction(3)
    T3, V42.
    T4, V10,21.
    T5, V7,8.
    T6, V8,21.
    T7, V1.
    T15, V11,18(2),20(2),21(2).

Mystery - Doreal's Introduction(1)
    T8, V4.
    T9, V18.
    T10, V3(3),6,10,20.
    T11, V6.
    T13, V2(2).
    T14, V6(2),14,15(2),16,31,36.
    T15, V4.

Secret(s)(ed)(ly) - Doreal's Introduction(5)
    T1, V5.
    T3, V29,30.
    T5, V14,17,30,31.
    T6, V6(2),14,17,18,19.
    T8, V5(2),17.
    T9, V15.
    T10, V4,24.
    T11, V2,5.
    T12, V22,24(2).
    T13, V3,4(2),5(2),10(2),13,14,24,25.
    T14, V3,4,5,15(2),36,42(2),43,48.
    T15, V1(2),9,17,19,25(2).

Thought(s) - Doreal's Introduction(2)
    T1, V17.
    T3, V41,42,43.
    T4, V4.
    T6, V21.
    T7, V25,29(2),30.
    T9, V24,35.
    T10, V1,7(2),8(4),17,33.
    T11, V4.
    T13, V14.
    T15, V20.

Vibration - Doreal's Introduction(2)
    T1, V22.
    T6, V21,25.

T8, V13.
T9, V4.
T10, V7.
T15, V14.

Water(s)(ed) - T1, V18(2),19,20,24.
   T10, V25.

Word(s) - Doreal's Introduction(4)
   T1, V6,17(3),22.
   T2, V20,28.
   T3, V14,35.
   T4, V20,22.
   T5, V7.
   T6, V11,23.
   T7, V12(2).
   T8, V4,9,17,32.
   T9, V3,19,28(4),30(3),31,32(2),33(3),34(2).
   T10, V9,10,17(2),18(2),19(2),35.
   T11, V1,2(2),25.
   T12, V1,9.
   T13, V1(2),15.
   T14, V42,44,45.
   T15, V1,15,18,21,23,24,25.

NOTES

Chapter Seventeen

Index of Power Prayers

Prayer for Aid from the Seven Lords

T6, V24.
By their names I call them to aid me,
free me and save me from the darkness of night:
UNTANAS, QUERTAS, CHIETAL,
and GOYANA, HUERTAL, SEMVETA-ARDAL.
By their names I implore thee,
free me from darkness
and fill me with LIGHT.

Prayer of Thoth

T12, V24-25.
Receive thou my blessing.
Take thou my way and follow the Light.
Blend thou thy Soul in the Great Essence.
ONE with the Great Light let thy consciousness be.
Call thou on me when thou dost need me.
Use my name three times in a row:
CHEQUETET, ARELICH, VOMALITES.

NOTES

Chapter Eighteen

Index of Power Words

Below are listed the Power Words that can be used daily.

There are other power words that are associated with certain techniques and should not be used lightly.

You will find those words listed under "Sacred Techniques."

Be sure you have purified yourself by "going within" before attempting any of the more advanced techniques.

The Names of the Seven Lords are Power Words in themselves:
UNTANAS, QUERTAS, CHIETAL, and GOYANA, HUERTAL, SEMVETA-ARDAL.

The sacred names of Thoth are Power Words:
CHEQUETET, ARELICH, VOMALITES.

Index of Power Words

T5, V7.
YTOLAN is a power word:
Out of the ETHER called HE its substance, molded and formed by the power of YTOLAN.

T10, V19.
ZIN-URU is a power word:
Hark ye, now man, this word I leave with thee.
Use it and ye shall find power in its sound.
Say ye, the word:
"ZIN-URU"
and power ye shall find.

NOTES

Chapter Nineteen

Index of Techniques

These techniques are divided into two categories:

Category One Techniques are good to be used often and help you to develop spiritually.

Category Two Techniques are only for the more advanced student.

Be sure you have purified yourself and feel guided before attempting any of the more advanced techniques of Category Two.

To attempt any of the advanced techniques before sufficient practice of the Category One techniques will only bring you failure and frustration.

Category One

Balance of Poles (Find a shorter version of this under the Meditation section.)

T13, V13.
List ye, O man, whilst I give the secret
so that ye, too, shalt taste not of change.
One hour each day shalt thou lie with thine head
pointed to the place of the positive pole (north).
One hour each day shalt thy head be pointed
to the place of the negative pole (south).
Whilst thy head is placed to the northward,
hold thou thy consciousness
from the chest to the head.

T13, V14.
And when thy head is placed southward,
hold thou thy thought from the chest to the feet.
Hold thou in balance once in each seven,
and thy balance will retain the whole of its strength.
Aye, if thou be old, thy body will freshen
and thy strength will become as a youth's.
This is the secret known to the Masters
by which they hold off the fingers of Death.
Neglect not to follow the path I have shown,
for when thou hast passed beyond years to a hundred
to neglect it will mean the coming of Death.

Technique to be free from darkness or dark influence

T6, V21.
*When unto thee there comes a feeling,
drawing thee nearer to the dark gate,*

*examine thine heart and find if the feeling
thou hast has come from within.
If thou shalt find the darkness thine own thoughts,
banish them forth from the place in thy mind.
Send through thy body a wave of vibration,
irregular first and regular second,
repeating time after time until free.
Start the WAVE FORCE in thy BRAIN CENTER.
Direct it in waves from thine head to thy foot.*

T6, V22.
*But if thou findest thine heart is not darkened,
be sure that a force is directed to thee.
Only by knowing can thou overcome it.
Only by wisdom can thou hope to be free.
Knowledge brings wisdom and wisdom is power.
Attain and ye shall have power o'er all.*

T6, V23.
*Seek ye first a place bound with darkness.
Place ye a circle around about thee.
Stand erect in the midst of the circle.
Use thou this formula, and thou shalt be free.
Raise thou thine hands to the dark space above thee.
Close thou thine eyes and draw in the LIGHT.
Call to the SPIRIT OF LIGHT through the Space-Time,
using these words and thou shalt be free:
"Fill thou my body, O SPIRIT OF LIFE,
fill thou my body with SPIRIT OF LIGHT.
Come from the FLOWER*

that shines through the darkness.
Come from the HALLS where the Seven Lords rule.
Name them by name, I, the Seven:
THREE, FOUR, FIVE,
and SIX, SEVEN, EIGHT-NINE.

T6, V24.
By their names I call them to aid me,
free me and save me from the darkness of night:
UNTANAS, QUERTAS, CHIETAL,
and GOYANA, HUERTAL, SEMVETA ARDAL.
By their names I implore thee,
free me from darkness
and fill me with LIGHT."

T6, V25.
Know ye, O man, that when ye have done this,
ye shall be free from the fetters that bind ye,
cast off the bondage of the BROTHERS of NIGHT.
See ye not that the names have the power
to free by vibration the fetters that bind?
Use them at need to free thou thine brother
so that he, too, may come forth from the night.

> Commentary: This is referring to the names of the seven Lords:
>
> UNTANAS, QUERTAS, CHIETAL, and GOYANA, HUERTAL, SEMVETA, ARDAL.

Category Two
Remember to heed the warning and only use these after advanced study of the Tablets and regular use of the balance of poles.

Technique to pass from your body at time of Death.
Passing in peace and RETAINING all the memories of this lifetime unto the next.

T13, V16.
Hear ye, O man, and list to my voice.
List to the wisdom that gives thee of Death.
When at the end of thy work appointed,
thou may desire to pass from this life,
pass to the plane where the Suns of the Morning live and have being as Children of Light.
Pass without pain and pass without sorrow
into the plane where is eternal Light.

T13, V17.
First lie at rest with thine head to the eastward.
Fold thou thy hands at the Source of thy life
(solar plexus).

T13, V18.
Place thou thy consciousness in the life seat.
Whirl it and divide to north and to south.

Index of Techniques

T13, V19.
Send thou the one out toward the northward.
Send thou the other out to the south.

T13, V20.
Relax thou thy hold upon thy being.
Forth from thy form will thy silver spark fly,
upward and onward to the Sun of the morning,
blending with Light, at one with its source.

T13, V21.
There it shall flame till desire shall be created.
Then shall return to a place in a form.

T13, V22.
Know ye, O men,
that thus pass the great Souls,
changing at will from life unto life.
Thus ever passes the Avatar,
willing his Death as he wills his own life.

T13, V23.
{The key to the placing of consciousness
at the time of death so that memory may be carried
from one incarnation to another.}

T13, V24.
List ye, O man, drink of my wisdom.
Learn ye the secret that is Master of TIME.

Index of Techniques

*Learn ye how those ye call Masters
are able to remember the lives of the past.*

T13, V25.
*Great is the secret yet easy to master,
giving to thee the mastery of time.
When upon thee death fast approaches,
fear not but know ye are master of Death.*

T13, V26.
*Relax thy body, resist not with tension.
Place in thy heart the flame of thy Soul.
Swiftly then sweep it to the seat of the triangle.*

T13, V27.
*Hold for a moment, then move to the goal.
This, thy goal, is the place between thine eyebrows,
the place where the memory of life must hold sway.*

T13, V28.
*Hold thou thy flame here in thy brain-seat
until the fingers of Death grasp thy Soul.
Then as thou pass through the state of transition,
surely the memories of life shall pass, too.*

T13, V29.
*Then shall the past be as one with the present.
Then shall the memory of all be retained.
Free shalt thou be from all retrogression.
The things of the past shall live in today.*

T13, V30.
Man, ye have heard the voice of my wisdom.
Follow, and ye shall live through the ages as I.

Technique to astral travel (Passing the barriers of space)

T15, V14.
On Earth, man is in bondage,
bound by space and time to the earth plane.
Encircling each planet, a wave of vibration,
binds him to his plane of unfoldment.
Yet within man is the Key to releasement,
within man may freedom be found.

T15, V15.
When ye have released the self from the body,
rise to the outermost bounds
of your earth-plane.
Speak ye the word DOR-E-UL-LA.
Then for a time your Light will be lifted,
free may ye pass the barriers of space.

T15, V16.
For a time of half of the sun (six hours),
free may ye pass the barriers of earth-plane,
see and know those who are beyond thee.
Yea, to the highest worlds may ye pass.
See your own possible heights of unfoldment,
know all earthly futures of Soul.

T15, V17.
Bound are ye in your body,
but by the power ye may be free.
This is the Secret whereby bondage
shall be replaced by freedom for thee.

T15, V18.
Calm let thy mind be.
At rest be thy body:
Conscious only of freedom from flesh.
Center thy being on the goal of thy longing.
Think over and over that thou wouldst be free.
Think of this word LA-UM-I-L-GAN-
over and over in thy mind let it sound.
Drift with the sound to the place of thy longing.
Free from the bondage of flesh by thy will.

Technique to enter the Halls of Amenti

T15, V19.
Hear ye while I give the greatest of secrets:
how ye may enter the Halls of Amenti,
enter the place of the immortals as I did,
stand before the Lords in their places.

T15, V20.
Lie ye down in rest of thy body.
Calm thy mind so no thought disturbs thee.
Pure must ye be in mind and in purpose,
else only failure will come unto thee.

T15, V21.
Vision Amenti as I have told in my Tablets.
Long with fullness of heart to be there.
Stand before the Lords in thy mind's eye.
Pronounce the words of power I give (mentally);
MEKUT-EL-SHAB-EL HALE-ZUR-BEN-EL-ZABRUT ZIN-EFRIM-QUAR-EL.
Relax thy mind and thy body.
Then be sure your soul will be called.

Technique to enter Shamballa

T15, V22.
Now give I the Key to Shamballa,
the place where my Brothers live in the darkness:
Darkness but filled with Light of the Sun -
Darkness of Earth, but Light of the Spirit,
guides for ye when my day is done.

T15, V23.
Leave thou thy body as I have taught thee.
Pass to the barriers of the deep, hidden place.
Stand before the gates and their guardians.
Command thy entrance by these words:

T15, V24.
"I am the Light. In me is no darkness.
Free am I of the bondage of night.
Open thou the way of the Twelve and the One,

so I may pass to the realm of wisdom."
When they refuse thee, as surely they will,
command them to open by these words of power:

T15, V25.
"I am the Light.
For me are no barriers.
Open, I command, by the Secret of Secrets -
EDOM-EL-AHIM-SABBERT-ZUR ADOM."
Then if thy words have been "Truth"
of the highest,
open for thee the barriers will fall.

NOTES

Chapter Twenty

Meditations Inspired by the Emerald Tablets

This chapter contains two meditations. If you prefer to LISTEN, visit: http://rebeccamarina.com/resources

    A. Shortie Balance of Poles and Chakra Clearing Meditation

    B. Flower of Fire Meditation

Shortie Balance of Poles and Chakra Clearing

This exercise is inspired by the Balance of Poles recommended in the Emerald Tablets.

Tablet 13, Verse 13,14,15.

Thoth recommends doing this exercise for two hours each day. Hey, these beings lived for thousands of years. Most of us don't have two hours to spend doing this exercise. In case you feel critical of yourself for that, please stop judging yourself. All effort is rewarded.

Meditations Inspired

I have (with permission) created a shorter version that strengthens the chakra systems as well. We have made use of the powers of the Seven Lords in addition to the Balance of the Poles. Remember the Seven Lords represent frequencies of the highest order. When you call out their names, their energies are present with you.

Lie with your head pointed to the North Pole. (Positive)

Place your consciousness from the chest (Heart) to the head.

Touch lightly your Heart chakra and say the word Goyana 7 times.

Then touch your Throat chakra and say the word Chietal 7 times.

Now touch your Third Eye chakra and say the word Quertas 7 times.

Next, touch your Crown and say the word Untanas 7 times.

Next touch your Alta Major chakra and say the word Thoth 7 times.
(The Alta Major chakra is located at the point where the head joins the neck.)

Meditations Inspired

Lie quietly and imagine that you can FEEL the magnetic earth energies balancing you to the positive pole.

Switch your position so that your head is now pointing to the South Pole. (Negative)

Place your consciousness from the chest (Heart) to the feet.

Touch lightly your Heart chakra and say the word Goyana 7 times.

Touch your Solar Plexus chakra and say the word Huertal 7 times.

Touch your Sexual chakra and say the word SemVeta 7 times.

Touch your Root chakra and say the word Ardal 7 times.

You will notice that you have done the Heart chakra twice. This is because the heart is the beginning and ending of all wisdom. (Tablet 3, V7.)

Lie quietly and imagine that you can FEEL the magnetic earth energies balancing you to the negative pole.

Take your time and when you feel ready, get up and go about your normal activities. You will be recharged and refreshed.

"Flower of Fire" Inner Earth Meditation

Prefer to listen?
Get this meditation audio FREE at:
www.rebeccamarina.com/resources

In the Emerald Tablets...
Flame is mentioned 55 times.
Fire is mentioned 42 times.
Flower is mentioned 16 times and almost always in union with Fire or Flame.

In preparation, please locate and touch your Alta Major chakra.
The Alta Major chakra is the "gateway to receiving" located at the juncture of where the back of the head meets the neck. It is associated with the Atlas, the first **cervical vertebra.**

Meditations Inspired

Please relax as you listen to the following words...

To begin this meditation, I read from the Emerald Tablets. Certain passages inspired me to create this meditation for you. The passages are as follows:

T7, V13.
Once said THEY unto me:
"O man, wouldst thou gain wisdom?
Seek for it in the heart of the flame.
Wouldst thou gain knowledge of power?
Seek ye it in the heart of the flame.
Wouldst be one with the heart of the flame?
Seek then within thine own hidden flame."

T8, V7.
Search ye the mysteries of Earth's heart.
Learn of the LAW that exists,
holding the stars in their balance
by the force of the primordial mist.

T8, V8.
Seek ye the flame of the EARTH'S LIFE.
Bathe in the glare of its flame.
Follow the three-cornered pathway
until thou, too, art a flame.

T8, V9.
Speak thou in words without voice
to those who dwell down below.

Enter the blue-litten Temple
and bathe in the fire of all life.

T8, V10.
Know, O man, thou art complex,
a being of earth and of fire.
Let thy flame shine out brightly.
Be thou only the fire.

Relax.

Do not fear the dark, but find a pearl of wisdom there.

Begin by calling in a circle of Protective Light all around you.

Begin now to relax your feet and your legs.

Tell your conscious mind to relax as your spirit mind is on alert.

You are absorbing this wisdom.

You are listening here for the purpose of transformation. Your heart is ever seeking, ever growing.

And as you hear these words, you are consumed by the fire of desire for spiritual advancement.

Relax your hips.

Relax your spine. All the muscles of your spine are relaxed.

Your shoulders relax.

Your neck relaxes, and your head begins to feel heavy.

Relax your jaw. Relax the muscles in your face.

Relax your chest muscles, next your abdomen.

Relax your pelvic floor.

Allow your legs to be spread slightly, if that is comfortable.

For a moment, put your awareness on your Alta Major, the forgotten chakra.

See this chakra as pulsating with desire for this awakening and this remembering.

Thoth begins to speak:

Take my hand, beloved, for thou hast honored me deeply by the great journey you have taken, to come into this physical existence at all.

Reveal I now, one of the secrets not known since the time of Atlantis - the secret of inner earth.

Come now as I take you by the hand, casting a circle of light around you. The circle of light around me creates an infinity loop between us two. You are safe, and you are supported.

Come watch as I raise my staff.

Allow your imagination to run free with me, as we create together.

An opening appears in the side of the mountain, near the great pyramid which I built with my commands.

Thoth continues:

Down we go into the darkness. I am holding fast to your hand.

Closer to me you are drawn, feeling my strength, and knowing that all is well with you. Only a few are chosen to have this experience.

Moving downward now, further still, until we come to the first city of inner earth.

There dwell my brothers and sisters who escaped from Atlantis.

Relax.

Yes, they have propagated their species and their civilization, bringing many of the secrets with them. Never before has this wisdom been revealed in this way.

I, Thoth, am the portal master. This pathway can only be opened by me, and that by invitation only.

Transformation and knowledge are not for those who have no thirst for wisdom.

Not all can be trusted.

Not all can be trusted to keep my secrets, for it is not wise to give powerful secrets to those who are foolish. I charge you, my beloved, to keep this knowledge to yourself, for you have sacrificed. You have heard the call.

Learn to discern those who are ready for more Light from the merely curious.

Those who would scoff, will not see any Light within this meditation...so let it be.

Relax.

Thoth continues:

The portal is now open.

With your hand still safely in mine, you now see a blue light glistening in the distance. You begin to hear the sounds of chanting by a thousand priests and priestesses.

Drums are softly playing, resonating with your beating heart!

The vibration is so high that your feet are no longer touching the earth. You're holding to my hand to keep from floating completely off. Your lips begin to tremble as you begin to feel the power of the vibrations coming from this place.

You move closer, and you see that this is indeed a Temple, fully illuminated with Sacred blue light.

The chanting continues.

As we move through the Temple, we see an altar, whereupon burns the flame of eternal life.

Few have entered this portal.

Few have been invited.

The priests and priestesses now lower the tone of their chanting till it's almost a whisper. You strive to hear the words they are saying and yet, you cannot make them out. This is not for you to know at this time.

When you receive revelation of the sacred word, it will only be after much striving. And when you do discover that one sacred word, you must keep it to yourself, for it holds within itself the keys of life and death.

Strive not for those things which are of no value to you at this point in your life. Ask for the wisdom that will further your soul purpose, and bring you great joy and happiness.

Thoth continues:

A hush now falls upon the crowd as, still holding fast to your hand, I lead you towards the altar.

Upon the altar there is a huge blue lotus flower. I wave my staff over the flower.

It ignites into a beautiful roaring flame of blue, purple, violet, and yellow, with only a few hints of red.

Relax.

This is the cleansing fire that will transform what you consider to be your iniquities.

This fire will transform even those things that are hidden from you.

Yes, the fire will transform your blockages at the rate that is most beneficial for you. For beloved, instant transformation is available, yet your physical being could not assimilate it.

And so I ask you, beloved, drop to your heart and ask yourself,"Am I ready for this "flower of fire" baptism?"

And if your answer is yes, then let us move forward.

Now step into the very center of this blue lotus flame. Feel the heat coming up through your feet, up through your legs, up through your loins, up through your abdomen, burning away all that causes you harm.

The flame moves up through your heart. Up through your spinal column fluid, setting you on fire. Upwards through your neck, into your head cavity, out your ears, out your eyes, bursting forth through your crown.

Become the flame, beloved. Allow yourself to be transformed into this flame. Yes, merge with this flame of transformation.

Feel yourself tingling all over with holy fire!

Know that I, Thoth, am supporting you. I will not leave you. Feel the relief, as so much pain is consumed by this fire.

Doubt of your own self-worth, doubt of your purpose, is consumed by this fire. See yourself as truly the light being that you are.

And now all the beings, the priests and priestesses, lock their arms together in concentric circles all around you.

The flames slowly begin to die. You fall to your knees, not in worship of anyone, but in gratitude for this work that is done in your DNA and your energy body for your soul's growth.

Allow yourself to be in the reverence, absorbing the energy and the love of these people, your brothers and sisters. Many of them were the high priests and priestesses of Atlantis. Some from what you might consider the mythical garden of Eden.

You rest now, with me, Thoth, by your side, after this most sacred cleansing ritual. We are in the very center of the eight concentric circles formed by the still softly chanting priests and priestesses.

The nearest circle is comprised of priestesses moving counter-clockwise. The next circle is of priests, moving clockwise. The next six circles then alternate, their movements in rhythm, with their continuing chant of joy and celebration for your amazing transformation.

I, Thoth, do now give you this blessing in an ancient dialect that your ears may not understand, and yet your heart cries for more. Zin Uru, Zin Uru, Zin Uru, Ytolan, Ytolan, Ytolan.

(Zin Uru sounds like zin-oo-roo.)

(Ytolan sounds like ee-tow-lon.)

Receive. Receive. Receive. Be blessed.

Let it be okay, beloved, not to understand all that has transpired. Yet know from this moment forward, certain elements of your being are forever transformed.

There is no going back. Some of you may have experienced great difficulty in doing this meditation. This is partly because an unconscious part of you knew that once you had this experience, there could be no going back.

On a subconscious level, perhaps you worried that you would not be able to handle the responsibility of more Light.

Yet know for a truth, even as it says in the Christian holy scriptures, you will not be burdened with more than you can bear.

This meditation is a gift of joy, my beloved, and this gift of joy is for You.

You cannot give out joy, unless you are joy.

Thoth continues:

As I look at so many light workers, I see that there is give, give, give, give, give. And beloved, you are dry, dry, dry, dry, dry. Come to the water. Come to the well and drink of the water.

And now seven priests approach you - Seven Lords. You may recognize them, the Lords of the seven frequencies.

Untanas, Quertas, Chietal, Goyana, Huertal, Sem-Veta, Ardal.

Each Lord has for you, a cup of Sacred Elixir.

Each of the seven Lords stands before you, and gives you to drink. Each Lord gives you a different, yet higher, frequency. Drink deeply as the Sacred Elixirs are offered.

Drink from the cup of Untanas.

Drink from the cup of Quertas.

Drink from the cup of Chietal.

Drink from the cup of Goyana.

Drink from the cup of Huertal.

Drink from the cup of SemVeta.

Drink from the cup of Ardal.

Rest in the love. Be the love. You are loved. You are LOVE.

And now it is time to leave this place - transformed forever.

You may feel like resting after this meditation, for you have burned away much that has stopped you from moving forward with confidence and ease.

Still holding my hand, I lead you gently from this place. There is complete silence as we leave. Not a sound is to be heard except the beating of your own heart.

And as you keep hold of my hand, you feel my pulse beating in rhythm with your own. I slowly guide you to the surface of the earth. I lead you to the shade of an enormous tree, where the branches part to allow you to enter.

The roots of the tree provide a wonderful bed for you to lie upon. Lie down and rest. It has been my honor to meet with you again, my friend, for you know that we are not strangers.

Lie and rest. Lie and rest. Let all these changes assimilate into your being. Lie and rest. You are loved. You are loved. You are honored. And as you rest, if you feel that you need to drift into a light slumber for a while, allow your body to do so, in order to recover from the great transformation that has occurred. Resting, relaxing. All is well.

NOTES

Chapter Twenty-one

How Thoth Built the Great Pyramid

The following explanation is according to Dr. Doreal, the pioneer who retrieved and translated the Emerald Tablets.

Below his words are the referring texts from the Emerald Tablets themselves.

The entrance to Amenti is below the Great Pyramid of Cheops (or Khufu). **This was built by changing the atomic structure of stone until it became very light. Then after it was in place, changing it back again.**

Beneath the Great Pyramid is the force-chamber, connected with the apex of the pyramid by a central shaft or well. In the upper portion of the shaft, is a lens or crystal through which rays from the force-chamber are directed.

These rays are bent into time-space. They continue curving open, into a dimensional pathway from beneath the pyramids, to the Halls of Amenti.

How Thoth Built the Great Pyramid

The Great Pyramid is indestructible. If its inner parts were disturbed, forces would be let loose by the guardians, which would destroy anyone or anything which came against it.

Below are the references from the Tablets themselves:

T1, V25.
Great grew the sons of KHEM,
conquering the people around them,
growing slowly upwards in Soul force.
Now for a time I go from among them
into the dark halls of Amenti,
deep in the halls of the Earth,
before the Lords of the Powers,
face to face once again with the Dweller.

T1, V26.
Raised I high over the entrance, a doorway,
a gateway leading down to Amenti.
Few there would be with courage to dare it,
few pass the portal to dark Amenti.
Raised over the passage, I, a mighty pyramid, using the power that overcomes Earth force (*gravity*).

Deep and yet deeper placed I
a force-house or chamber;
from it carved I a circular passage
reaching almost to the great summit.
There in the apex, set I the crystal,

sending the ray into the "Time-Space,"
drawing the force from out of the ether,
concentrating upon the gateway to Amenti.
(See "The Great Pyramid" by Doreal.)

T1, V27.
Other chambers I built
and left vacant to all seeming,
yet hidden within them are the keys to Amenti.
He who in courage would dare the dark realms,
let him be purified first by long fasting.
Lie in the sarcophagus of stone in my chamber.
Then reveal I to him the great mysteries.
Soon shall he follow to where I shall meet him,
even in the darkness of Earth shall I meet him,
I, Thoth, Lord of Wisdom,
meet him and hold him and dwell with him always.

T1, V28.
Builded I the Great Pyramid,
patterned after the pyramid of Earth force,
burning eternally so that it, too,
might remain through the ages.
In it, I builded my knowledge of "Magic-Science"
so that it might be here
when again I return from Amenti.
Aye, while I sleep in the Halls of Amenti,
my Soul roaming free will incarnate,
dwell among men in this form or another.
(Hermes, thrice-born.)

NOTES

Chapter Twenty-two

Are You A Keymaster of the Emerald Tablets?

From the author, Rebecca: Thoth has expressed to me his interest in gathering together his Keymasters from around the globe.

Q. What is a Keymaster?

- A. A Keymaster is a person who has some part in helping bring these teachings of The Emerald Tablets to life.

Q. How does one know if they are a Keymaster?

- A. If you are interested in The Emerald Tablets and you are not sure why...you are likely one of the Keymasters to whom Thoth is referring.

- B. If you feel fascinated with Atlantis, Egypt or ancient mysteries, you are likely a Keymaster.

It is not necessary to understand WHY you have this fascination... simply be open to the concept.

Thoth explains that many have made soul agreements to be a part of the evolution of humanity by bringing forth the vibration of the Emerald Tablets.

Each Keymaster has a part in raising this awareness. Some have very large parts, some smaller parts.

Each part is equal in importance!

Doreal was a Keymaster, who went to great lengths to retrieve the Tablets and translate them.

Your part could be as simple as reading the Tablets, and bringing that vibration into this dimension.

This author's part is to format these Tablets into chapter and verse, for ease of study and reference.

It is also this author's part to hold Keymaster gatherings when guided.

At a Keymaster event, you can expect to feel more solid in your role as Keymaster. You can expect to find direction and feel confident.

It will be like a homecoming to your own personal truth.

You can also expect to learn how to channel the wisdom of Thoth directly.

For information on the next Keymaster Gathering visit: www.rebeccamarina.com/resources

Gatherings are live events and are also live-streamed to allow world-wide attendance.

NOTES

Chapter Twenty-three

Thoth on Judgment

Thoth the Atlantean, author of The Emerald Tablets, sought wisdom throughout all of his lifetimes.

In reading the Emerald Tablets, I noticed that every time Thoth was going to do something really important, or make a shift forward in consciousness, he would fast.

Thoth would go without food and water, denying himself many things. This would give him more focus to do the deep Spirit work that he was preparing to do.

An especially powerful example, was when Thoth abstained from food and water for several days, in preparation to pass through the purifying fire. He did so seven times, then seven times more. This was one of his most heroic acts, as Thoth did this in order to conquer the Dark Lords, who held captive the Lady of Light.

Thoth on Judgment

In Tablet 10, V 21 Thoth tells us:
Called I from the other planes of being,
one who was fairer than the daughters of men.
Aye, I called her from out of the spaces
to shine as a Light in the world of men.

> In my opinion, this refers to Thoth bringing forth from captivity, the Divine Feminine.
>
> (Read the complete account of rescuing the Lady of Light. Tablet 10, V 21 to 27.)

Because fasting is important to Thoth, I asked him "Should students fast from food for two or three days, in order to understand the Tablet teachings more fully?"

Thoth replied, "Rebecca, what people need to fast from, more than food, is...JUDGMENT!

It is very detrimental to spiritual growth to have a lot of judgment.

People don't realize how the judgment they're receiving, giving out, and especially the self-judgment, is stopping their deeper understanding.

So, Rebecca, ask students to refrain from judging themselves and others, for at least three days, before asking for any big leaps forward in spiritual growth."

Thoth on Judgment

Wouldn't you love to have a free pass for non-judgment?

This will take some doing.

For the next three days, every time you notice that you're starting to judge, just remember, "Oh, free pass. Non-judgment day. Today, I don't judge myself. Today, I don't judge others. Today, I live in the freedom of the moment. And so it is."

How could you apply this to your life?

Doesn't it sound like something that you're longing to do?

When you give up judgment...you will have a lot more brain space available!

Your heart will feel lighter.

There will be a lot less NOISE in your consciousness!

Now, you can finally hear that still small voice!

Now you can focus on those things which bring you joy!

I sent an email to my list of readers, inviting them to partake in three days of non-judgment.

Many reported back to me that it was HARDER to NOT judge themselves, than to NOT judge others.

Thank you, Thoth, for this guidance!

NOTES

References

The Brotherhood of the White Temple. This Church, founded by M. Doreal in the 1930's, is based on the Universal Brotherhood of Man. Gratitude to the Brotherhood for making this material available.

Find many other books by Doreal here: https://brotherhoodofthewhitetemple.com/

Drunvalo Melchizedek: Founder - The School of Remembering.

Author of **The Ancient Secret of the Flower of Life, Vol. I and II, Serpent of Light, Living in the Heart, and more.**

Drunvalo teaches about Thoth and The Emerald Tablets, and is a trusted source of information. Watch his specials on Gaia.com

https://www.drunvalo.net/

Billy Carson: Author of "Compendium of The Emerald Tablets, A Beginners Guide"

See his specials on Gaia.com

Billy Carson has done extensive research on The Emerald Tablets and Thoth. His book is excellent, and will give you even more insight into The Emerald Tablets.

Billy Carson is one of the most impressive people I have ever watched on Gaia. Information comes forth from him that is truly amazing! He is very knowledgeable about this topic, and many others.
https://www.4biddenknowledge.com/bio

The Gaia network:
https://www.gaia.com This is an internet based network on Metaphysics, spiritual truths, secret space programs, yoga, ancient mysteries and more. Highly recommended.

Rebecca's homepage:
http://www.rebeccamarina.com Find information on live events, online classes, new portal openings, channeled messages, private and group sessions. You may book Rebecca for a speaking engagement live or online.

Rebecca's YouTube channel:
www.youtube.com/HPTfree Over 400 videos and messages to help you.

About the Author

Rebecca considers her greatest accomplishment, the birthing and raising of her five children, and then adopting a sixth. When asked "Why so many?" She jokingly replies..."I only meant to have one!"

Raised as the daughter of an evangelical minister, Rebecca had to overcome a lot of religious fears and programming to find her own voice. At the ripe old age of 40, the Archangel Gabriel paid Rebecca a visit, which changed her life forever!

The message from Gabriel was crystal clear...teach people, so that they too, can call upon the Angels of God. Regardless of status or feelings of unworthiness, all people are equal and able to be heard.

> For the complete story of the Archangel Gabriel visit http://rebeccamarina.com/resources

Years later, through a miraculous sequence of events, Rebecca was called upon to be a "Portal Master."

About the Author

She has traveled to many places in the world, in answer to Spirit, to open portals for various reasons. One portal was on a battlefield, to open a space for trapped souls to exit. Another was in Jamaica, to open a pathway for the return of Unicorn magic. Another was in Costa Rica, to open the Anti-war portal for more angelic assistance to help suppress the bloodlust now prevalent on the Earth.

The most complex portal was in South Carolina, which was the "Portal of Transmutation." This portal is used for the purpose of giving every spirit a chance to make a choice. Many dark spirits are being given a chance to choose the Light. Calling for the Portal of Transmutation, gives them a chance to be taken to a place of neutrality, so that they may see both sides, in order to facilitate their choice.

When Spirit calls her, with explicit instructions for a new portal opening...Rebecca answers the call.

At present, she is committed to opening a portal that allows better understanding of The Emerald Tablets.

Rebecca is a most gifted channel, medium, and healer. She believes that EVERYONE has the capacity to develop these gifts. She often teaches classes on channeling, mediumship, and developing your own psychic/intuitive gifts. Rebecca has been quoted as saying: "Give me a left-brained engineer, and if he/

About the Author

she will simply follow my instructions, they will be talking to the Spirit world in no time at all."

She currently resides in South Texas, near her beloved Gulf of Mexico.

Contact Rebecca through her website: www.rebeccamarina.com or email her at Rebecca@rebeccamarina.com

www.ingramcontent.com/pod-product-compliance
Lightning Source LLC
Chambersburg PA
CBHW030438300426
44112CB00009B/1059